Oranges and Lemons

By the same author

How to Choose the Right Craft for You - 2017

Playing *Oranges and Lemons*

Oranges and Lemons

. . . and other citrus fruit – their history, uses and impact on human culture and health

ISBN: 978-1-9999281-1-7

First published 2019

For all the teachers who inspired me with
a love of learning for its own sake

ST CLEMENT DANES

The church of St Clement Danes in London's Strand holds a special lunchtime Oranges and Lemons service each year on the third Thursday in March, as it has done ever since 1920. This service commemorates the reference to the church – or possibly that of St Clement Eastcheap – in the nursery rhyme *Oranges and Lemons.*

Children of St Clement Danes Primary School ring out *Oranges and Lemons*

In this photo children at the St Clement Danes Primary School are ringing out the nursery rhyme *Oranges and Lemons* on handbells in the nave of the church of St Clement Danes. After the service, each child is given an orange and a lemon to take home. This photo was taken at the 2019 service.

ORANGES AND LEMONS

Oranges and lemons,
Say the bells of St Clement's.

I owe you five farthings,
Say the bells of St Martin's.

When will you pay me?
Say the bells of Old Bailey.

When I grow rich,
Say the bells of Shoreditch.

When will that be?
Say the bells of Stepney.

I do not know,
Says the great bell of Bow.

Here comes the candle to light you to bed,
And here comes the chopper to chop off your head!

CONTENTS

LIST OF ILLUSTRATIONS

XXXVII	PLASTIC JUICE EXTRACTOR
XXXVIII	GLASS LEMON SQUEEZER (closed)
XXXIX	GLASS LEMON SQUEEZER (open)
XL	LARGE HAND CITRUS SQUEEZER
XLI	ELECTRIC CITRUS SQUEEZER FOR HOME USE
XLII	WOODEN REAMER
XLIII	GRATER
XLIV	CITRUS ZESTER
XLV	ROBERTSON'S GOLDEN SHRED
XLVI	ORANGE AND LEMON EXTRACT
XLVII	LIME PICKLE
XLVIII	JAFFA CAKES
XLIX	PURE ORANGE JUICE
L	TINNED MANDARIN SEGMENTS
LI	MANDARIN ORANGE SEGMENTS
LII	ANTIQUE HAND CITRUS SLICER FOR MARMALADE
LIII	HAND CITRUS SLICER FOR MARMALADE
LIV	SPLITTING ORANGES FOR MARMALADE
LV	CUTTING GRAPEFRUIT
LVI	GRAPEFRUIT KNIFE
LVII	GRAPEFRUIT SPOONS
LVIII	HALF GRAPEFRUIT WITH GLACÉ CHERRY
LIX	SELECTION OF ORANGE FLAVOURED CHOCOLATE
LX	LINDT LIME INTENSE
LXI	LINDT PINK GRAPEFRUIT
LXII	MOULES ET FRITES
LXIII	MACKEREL WITH ORANGE
LXIV	LEMON WITH OLIVE OIL SHORTBREAD
LXV	HOMEMADE LEMONADE
LXVI	LEMON FUDGE
LXVII	HOMEMADE LEMON CURD
LXVIII	GIN AND TONIC
LXIX	ARNOLFINI PORTRAIT

- o 0 o -

PREFACE

Oranges, lemons and other citrus fruit have long been far more than mere food. Today there is an ever-expanding list of varieties of citrus fruit, some arising by accident, while others have been carefully hybridised or engineered.

These fruit and their components have played a major part not just in recipes, but also in health, medicine, culture and many household uses.

It was not until the 16th Century that the colour orange, previously referred to as yellow-red, was given its own name. Once the fruit became readily available in Western Europe, the colour orange was firmly established in our language.

Lemon is still not generally regarded as a colour in its own right, usually being referred to as 'lemon yellow' or 'yellow colour'.

Oranges and Lemons looks at the role citrus fruit have played in history, their wide variety of uses, and how they have shaped the human diet, culture and health. It also touches on how the words *orange* and *lemon* have been used in a number of other fields with their subsequent influences on our lives and in history.

Chapter 1.
INTRODUCTION

The first encounter with a citrus grove, whether it is oranges, lemons or grapefruit, is a spectacular sight. With deep green leaves on evergreen trees, interspersed with fragrant, waxy white flowers and bright golden fruit glistening like jewels, it is a true piece of natural art. In addition, there is always the promise of a delicious harvest.

There are well over a thousand different types of citrus fruits. Although their precise history seems uncertain, it appears that originally there were only three species of citrus fruit – mandarin orange, pummelo (or Chinese grapefruit) and citron. However, there is some evidence that a fourth species, namely the papeda, may have played a part.

Despite producing an unpalatable fruit that is slow growing and bitter, some species of papeda are used in landscaping, while others are important as rootstock and for breeding disease-resistant and frost-hardy citrus hybrids. For example, the Key Lime, a hybrid between papeda, micrantha (*citrus hystrix*) and citron, has in turn, given rise to many commercial types of lime.

Citrus trees can be either notoriously promiscuous, or insular and self-fertile. For example, many types of lemon or satsuma do not need cross-pollination to set fruit. Most orange flowers are perfect, meaning they have both male and female parts. The female portion, the pistil, comprises the stigma, style and ovary, while the male part, the pollen-laden stamen, includes the filament and anthers. As a result many are self-fertile.

Although citrus are often fertilized by self-pollination, they will produce further varieties and sometimes more fruit with cross-pollination. Most of the countless varieties of cultivated oranges, lemons and other citrus fruit that exist today have arisen from the hybridisation, breeding and cross-pollination of the core ancestral types of citrus.

Tangerines, for example, are usually self-fertile, but some varieties are self-sterile, needing another tree to pollinate them. Clementines cannot pollinate themselves or the flowers of other clementine trees, but they can cross-pollinate with other citrus species. If clementine flowers are not pollinated, the fruit will be seedless.

Many citrus seeds tend to sprout a high proportion of nuclear, asexually produced seedlings with the same characteristics as the original seed. However, Persian limes are different as they produce may zygotic seedlings, that is, seedlings from a fertilised egg cell. Since zygotic seedlings from hybrid parents can resemble almost any kind of citrus fruit, the offspring of Persian limes can be unpredictable.

From a botanical standpoint, plants are classified in a family, then a genus, and then as an individual species. Citrus fruits belong to the Rutaceae family and the genus of flowering trees and shrubs, *Citrus*. Today, plants in this genus produce numerous types of citrus fruit, including oranges, lemons, grapefruits, pomelos and limes.

Many of us learned at school that plants or animals within an individual species can interbreed, but do not breed with another species, or if they did (such as a horse and an ass) the offspring would be infertile (as in the mule). This is no longer seen to be correct.

It is now known that some species can interbreed with other closely related species, producing hybrids or crosses that may be fertile. This is true of citrus, which carelessly reproduce easily, resulting in many crosses and mutations, some of which are natural, and others which are man-made.

In this regard, the relationship between limes and lemons is complex, with the smaller lime probably being a predecessor of the lemon. Although the origin is unclear, some sources say that the lemon, *citrus limon*, was developed in two stages, first as a hybrid between lime and citron, possibly in India or Pakistan, and then later as a hybrid between lime and pummelo in the Middle East.

Citrus fruit are now grown in many countries where there is a mild or tropical climate. They are eaten widely across the world, bringing nourishment in the form of Vitamin C, fibre and potassium, and helping to provide a healthy diet.

THE ORIGINS OF THE COLOURS ORANGE AND LEMON

The colour orange may be named after the appearance of the ripe orange fruit, but this can be misleading, as the ripeness of an orange is not indicated by its colour. If an orange is not picked, it can stay on the tree until the next season. During this time, fluctuations in temperature can make it turn from green to orange and back to green again without the quality or flavour being adversely affected.

The colour of an orange depends on where it grows. In more temperate climes, its green skin turns orange when the weather cools; but in countries where it's always hot, the chlorophyll is preserved in the skin, and the fruit can stay green. Vietnamese, Thai and Jamaican oranges are green-skinned while being ripe and orange inside.

The origins of the word 'orange' follow several historical trade and cultural routes. It appears to come from the ancient Sanskrit word *naranga*, meaning 'perfume within'.

It is also possibly derived from Dravidian, another ancient language spoken in what is now southern India, from a root, *naru*, meaning ‘fragrant’.

Along with the orange fruit, the word *nāranj* migrated into Persian and Arabic and passed through several other languages including Italian *arancia*, and Old French, *pomme d’orange*, before reaching English. The earliest uses of the word in English refer to the fruit, and orange was not used as a name for the colour until the 1540s.

Another possible source is Arausio, (or Orange) the name of a small city in south east France which was a principality in the Middle Ages, the descendants of which formed the House of Orange. *Arausio* is an ancient name for orange in French, but today it is called *orange* in France and Germany, and *oranje* in the Netherlands.

Naranja is the word for the orange in modern-day Spanish, and *laranja* is the Portuguese equivalent.

Buddhists associate the colour of the citrus tree fruit with devotees dressed in orange-red. Orange-red, being the colour of a flame, is worn symbolically by Buddhist monks who seek to burn all their desires.

The origins of the word *lemon* may be Middle Eastern. It draws from the Old French *limon*, then Italian *limone*, from the Arabic *laymūn* or *līmūn*, and from the Persian *līmūn*, a generic term for ‘citrus fruit’, which has the same origin as the Sanskrit (*nimbū*, ‘lime’).

Then there is lime green – the colour of a lime fruit, which is somewhere between chartreuse and lemon yellow.

Chapter 2.

BACKGROUND, HISTORY AND ORIGINS

Given the important role taken by citrus fruit in our lives, it is surprising that their origins and history are somewhat elusive and littered with many contradictory citations.

Perhaps the first known references to oranges were in China around 500 BC (BCE) by Confucius, although recent research indicates that citrus fruits originated in India and the foothills of the Himalayas, rather than in China.

Previously, they were believed to be native to the subtropical and tropical regions of Asia and the Malay Archipelago, along with that part of south east Asia bordered by north east India, Myanmar and the Yunnan province of China. It is this area where some species of oranges, mandarins, and lemons were first believed to be cultivated commercially.

CITRUS TRAVELLING WEST

Citrus fruit have been grown in an ever-widening area since ancient times. The ancestor of today's citrus trees, the citron (*citrus medica*) was brought west from India by Alexander the Great (356–323 BC (BCE)) and his armies, via Persia and the Middle East into Greece, Italy, Turkey, and North Africa in the late fourth Century BC (BCE).

The citron, one of the original four citrus species, was bred in the Middle East well before the cultivation of other citrus fruit. Often 10–15 cm (4–6 inches) long, it has a thick white pith, and although it is rarely eaten, it has many medicinal, cultural, cleansing and household applications.

The citron tree bears fruit all year round, with some ripening while others are still at the flowering stage or just beginning to change into fruit. This fruit was called the *Persian* or *Median apple*, and grew in Media (modern-day Azerbaijan, Kurdistan, and parts of Kermanshah) and Persia (modern-day Iran).

Citron, in the form of the fragrant yellow etrog, a lemon-like fruit with virtually no pulp, has been in the Middle East for millennia. The etrog, also called *Adam's apple*, or *paradise apple*, is possibly the original fruit of the Tree of Knowledge in the Garden of Eden.

As one of the first citrus fruits in the western world, the etrog became a vital article for Jews in some of their ritual celebrations. There are several ancient references to this unusual fruit.

Egyptologist and archaeologist Victor Loret claimed to have identified drawings of an etrog tree on the walls of the botanical garden at the Temple of Karnak near Luxor, Egypt, which dates back almost 3,000 years ago, although he admitted that the drawings were *not clear*.

Author and naturalist Pliny the Elder (23–79 AD (CE)) called the citron *nata Assyria malus* and saw its ugly fruit as remarkably bitter, but useful because of its strong odour, which repels moths.

A native of Lesbos, Greece, Theophrastos (371–287 BC (BCE)) is regarded as the father of botany for his work on plants. He referred to citron (*citrus medica*), or the Persian citrus, as having a wonderful perfume. It was not eaten, but put among clothes, for its pleasant fragrance while also being an insect repellent.

There is a phrase used in the Torah to describe the etrog as *pri etz hadar* or 'the fruit of a beautiful (hadar) tree'. While the individual fruits (lemon, orange, etc) do have their own names in modern Hebrew, the generic term for citrus fruit is *pri hadar*.

The Bible tells of the oppression of the Israelites as slaves in Egypt, their flight from that country led by Moses, and their journey through the wilderness before eventually they settled in the *Promised Land*.

The Hebrew people (the Children of Israel) had been born as slaves in Egypt. Moses tried to get the Pharaoh to liberate the Hebrew slaves, but he couldn't persuade him, so God sent 10 plagues to put pressure on the Pharaoh.

The plagues included turning the waters of the land of Egypt to blood; an invasion of frogs which covered the land; hordes of wild animals roaming Egypt, destroying everything in their path; and pestilence killing most of the domesticated animals. People were struck by painful boils, unprecedented hailstorms, swarms of locusts, death of their first-born and other torments.

So reluctantly the Pharaoh let the Hebrews go. Moses led his people into the wilderness to Mount Sinai, where he received the Ten Commandments. The Hebrew people roamed the desert for 40 years before they reached the *Promised Land.*

It is difficult to date this Exodus accurately, but in I Kings 6:1 there is a reference to King Solomon building his temple some 480 years after the flight, so it would appear to have been perhaps around 1450 BC (BCE). And the Israelites brought the citron etrog with them from Egypt to Israel.

Leviticus refers to the etrog as being one of the four species required for ritual use during the Feast of Tabernacles or Sukkot (Lev. 23:40). The others are the *lulav* (palm frond), *aravah* (willow), and *hadass* (a branch of myrtle). Sukkot comes five days after Yom Kippur and celebrates the gathering of the harvest. It commemorates the miraculous protection God provided for the Children of Israel in their Exodus from Egypt.

Passover is a spring-time Jewish festival when a special ritual meal, the Seder, commemorates God's liberation of the Jews from slavery in ancient Egypt under the leadership of Moses.

There are examples of the etrog in mosaic floors and frescoes in synagogues from the Roman and Byzantine period, and it is such an important Jewish icon that it is found on many ancient coins.

The etrog tree is very delicate, requiring much water and constant care. It starts to bear fruit after about five years, but because it is vulnerable to diseases, particularly those of the root system, it rarely lives more than 10 to 15 years. The solution, once the lemon appeared in the Mediterranean, was to graft an etrog onto a base of another citrus tree, most often a rough lemon rootstock, thus using the vigorous base of the lemon to nourish the etrog. A grafted citron tree, known as a *murkav*, is far more durable, having a life expectancy of 30 to 35 years, and requiring less care.

With an expanding Jewish population living in colder climates and away from the Middle East, the need to import the etrog from afar for ritual use became increasingly important. To serve this need, farmers in the Greek Ionian Islands, and in particular the islanders on Corfu, became experts at growing this interesting fruit. By the mid-18th Century etrog orchards in Corfu were shipping the fruit to many distant Sephardic lands.

However, there were increasing discussions as to whether the etrog from Greece was Kosher, given that it was a grafting of two plants. An etrog harvested from a tree that was grafted onto another species was soon seen as invalid for Sukkot use. Over time the market for the Greek etrog dwindled and etrog orchards in Italy, that were growing ungrafted trees, took over. The etrog is no longer exported from Greece for ritual purposes.

Farmers on the shores of Calabria at the very south of Italy have grown citron and ungrafted etrog for many centuries. This region has a microclimate with warm air from the sea meeting the cold mountain breezes, and also has fertile soil, creating an ideal habitat for these delicate trees.

Today the majority of etrogs are grown on ungrafted trees in Israel where orchards are known to be of untainted pedigree. They are then used locally and exported worldwide.

Calabria, with its history of supplying this special fruit, is still a source of 'pure bred' etrog but is less important than Israel. Each year during the summer harvest, several rabbis visit Calabria to inspect trees and select the best etrog. Rabbinical certification guarantees that these etrogs are Kosher. These are then sent to Jewish communities throughout the world.

Although citron has been in the Middle East and on the edges of the Mediterranean for several millennia, quickly followed by the etrog, other citrus fruits took considerably longer to arrive.

Limited numbers of sour oranges (*citrus aurantium*) along with lemons (*citrus limon*) were imported into Italy from India and China by the Romans in the first and second centuries AD (CE). However, they were not widely cultivated, and with the fall of the Roman Empire to the barbarians in 476 AD (CE), they all but disappeared except in some southern regions.

The Arabs brought lemons and sour oranges west along the Silk Road to Persia and then into Europe. They reintroduced them to Italy when they invaded Sicily in 831 AD (CE), revived the art of citriculture and brought Persian techniques of cultivation, planting and irrigation.

Until then, virtually the only citrus in Europe had been the citron, brought to Calabria by the Jews in about 70 AD (CE).

In the sixth and seventh Centuries the expanding forces of Islam conquered a wide corridor across the world from India to the Mediterranean. Orange, tangerine and lemon trees mark the track of the Muslim armies westward.

The Moors invaded Iberia in 711 AD (CE) ruling much of Spain and Portugal, and bringing citrus trees, including the sour orange, with them. The Berber-Hispanic Muslims initially inhabited two-thirds of the peninsula for 375 years, about half of it for another 160 years, and finally the Kingdom of Granada for a further 244 years.

At its height, Cordoba, the heart of the Moorish territory in Spain, was the most modern city in Europe, with well-paved streets, street-lamps and some 900 public baths. Moorish Spain was well in advance of the rest of Europe. Education was universal, while in Christian Europe 99 per cent of the population was illiterate.

During this occupation, northern Europe had just two universities, while the Moors had seventeen in the southern part of modern-day Spain. They introduced paper to Europe, and Arabic numerals which replaced the clumsy Roman system. The Moors also brought in many new crops such as saffron, fig, sugar cane, rice and much more, as well as oranges and lemons.

Moorish farmers improved the structure and fertility of the soil. Their techniques included distinguishing between different qualities of soil by the texture, colour and natural vegetation already growing there.

Details of how to improve fertility and soil structure were set out in the *Book of Agriculture*, a 34-chapter treatise written by Spanish Moor Ibn al-Awwam in the latter part of the 12th Century. Heavy clay was made more friable by digging in sand; sandy soil was given more body with the introduction of clay. Other additions included crushed bricks, rags and household compost, along with bird and animal dung.

However, Ibn al-Awwam had some strange ideas. He warned farmers to guard their citrus trees against visits from menstruating women, whose “mere presence would cause a total loss of both fruit and leaves. Women should not be allowed to come near citrus trees”. Following on in this denigratory vein, he also believed that “If a woman eats an orange, it will banish all evil thoughts from her mind” which speaks volumes for how much value he placed on citrus.

In addition to the larger groves of oranges and lemons introduced to Spain by the Moors, smaller numbers of citrus trees were planted in two spectacular pieces of Islamic architecture, the Great Mosque of Cordoba (La Mezquita) and the Alhambra Palace (literally ‘the red one’) in Granada, the latter of which still has oranges and lemons in the gardens today. The Alhambra was the seat of Muslim rulers from the 13th Century to the end of the 15th Century.

Christians and Catholics remained in Northern Spain, and periodically sought to recapture the south from the Moors. Toledo was regained in 1085, and Cordoba fell in 1236. One by one, the Moors’ strongholds surrendered. The last remaining

Moorish city, Granada, was recaptured by Ferdinand V and Isabella 1 in 1492, when the Muslim armies surrendered. Even today the many years of Moorish influence have left an unmistakable mark on southern Spain's architecture, music, art and view of life.

During the Middle Ages in Northern Europe pungent spices, sugar and citrus juices were generously used in prestigious menus to display wealth. In view of the climate, such crops could not be grown there and so had to be imported. As a result, they were extraordinarily expensive.

The number of oranges used at the table indicated the relative importance of the diners. A multi-course dinner that included citrus in various dishes, oranges, lemons and citron, in juices, slices and candied peels, demonstrated the high status of the guests.

By the 13th Century citrus fruit was reasonably common in Italy. With the expansion of the Islamic influences across the Mediterranean and the Christian soldiers returning from the Crusades, citrus spread throughout Southern Europe and North Africa.

Although there are some references to sweet oranges arriving in Genoa in the 15th Century, growers in Europe concentrated on cultivating bitter oranges until the beginning of the 16th Century because they were more aromatic and better for seasoning.

As trade routes opened up between Asia and Europe, the costs of spices diminished, and heavily spiced dishes lubricated with the juice of sour oranges lost their câchet. The Portuguese are usually credited with bringing the first sweet oranges from India to Europe when Vasco da Gama discovered the sea route around the Cape of Good Hope in 1498.

Italy became important as a source for lemons around the middle of the 15th Century, when the first substantial cultivation of lemons in Europe started in Genoa. Sour oranges were seen as hardy, but the lemons proved far more fragile, unable to cope with frost, drought, excessive heat or rain. But with effective irrigation systems, growing lemons became realistic, providing a reliable source of food and employment.

Father Alvaro Semmedo, a Portuguese Jesuit, went to the Far East and in 1640 wrote about oranges in Canton. He believed them to be infinitely superior to the Indian oranges already familiar to Europe via Portugal.

In the 16th Century, Portuguese ships returning from expeditions to China brought back orange trees. Their arrival in Europe coincided with a move by the wealthy to a simpler style of cooking.

The fruits of these trees from Canton were so sweet that they acquired the botanical name of *Citrus sinensis* ('sweet orange'). Locally, they quickly became known as Portuguese oranges, soon replacing the bitter orange still found in Seville today. So powerful was this switch that the word 'Portugal' is still used for sweet oranges in the Greek, Romanian, and Albanian languages.

From Europe, citrus crossed the Atlantic to the Americas. Christopher Columbus, under orders, took the first orange and lemon seeds and plants to the New World on his ship *Hispaniola* in his second voyage of 1493.

He then spread them to the Antilles and a range of other Caribbean islands. Each sailor on Spanish ships was required by Spanish law to carry 100 seeds with him. In case the seeds dried out, they also carried young trees, with the aim of establishing citrus for medical uses and decoration in the new colonies.

It seems likely that Spanish conquistador Juan Ponce de León introduced oranges to North America when he discovered Florida in 1513. He planted the first orange trees around St Augustine, Florida, in the mid-1500s, although substantial planting in both Florida and California didn't take place until the 19th Century.

Sir Francis Drake levelled the orange trees of St Augustine when he sacked the town in 1586, but the stumps put out new shoots and eventually bore fruit again, many being bitter oranges.

Jan van Riebeeck, the first Governor of the Dutch colony of Cape Town, South Africa, introduced oranges there in 1654, and in 1788 Captain Arthur Phillips, the first Governor of New South Wales, took oranges to Australia.

MEDICI

After the fall of the Roman Empire in the fifth century AD (CE), both scientific and scholarly advancement slowed greatly. But a Renaissance began when Italian scholars, scientists and artists created a cultural movement based on a return to classical sources of learning. Tuscany, and in particular Florence, provided the cradle of this Renaissance in the early 14th Century.

In the Neo-Latin era of the Renaissance, oranges were sometimes referred to as 'Medici', coming from the Greek word for citron or Median apple. It is not surprising, therefore, that the Medici dynasty adopted the orange tree as its family symbol, had oranges painted on ceilings in their palaces and became some of the earliest collectors of citrus trees. These collections were fashionable and popular with wealthy merchants in the 16th and 17th Centuries, with remarkable cross-bred citrus bringing great delight and status.

In 1544 the Medici created one of the greatest ever citrus gardens at the Villa di Castello. The gardens, with their citrus collection including many unusual and rare varieties, were intended to reflect the wealth and high social position of the family. Citrus trees were planted in pots, some with wheels, so they could be brought indoors during the cold winter months to protect them from frost.

When Gian Gastone de Medici died in 1737, his sister bequeathed the family's entire property, including its vast multi-generational collection of citrus trees, to Francis I, Duke of Lorraine, on condition that it should not be removed from Florence. His son, Pietro Leopoldo, was passionately interested in natural sciences and appreciated the enormous importance of preserving such an ancient and varied botanical collection along with numerous other items the Medici had acquired.

LA SPECOLA

The Florentine Museum, La Specola, was founded by Leopoldo in 1775, initially as the Royal Imperial Museum of Physics and Natural History. By amalgamating all his own *natural curiosities,* as well as the Medici ones, the enlightened Leopoldo planned to offer the people of Florence the opportunity to educate themselves.

This was one of the first museums in the world to be accessible to the general public. However, initially a distinction was made between the lower classes, who could enter between 8 and 10 am, "if decently dressed", and the intelligent and well educated, who had free access from 1 o'clock as long as they removed their swords and overcoats, and left them by the door.

In subsequent years, the museum became popularly known by the Florentine people as *La Specola*, the name for the astronomical observatory located in its tower, which was built in 1789. The Boboli Gardens, a fantastic open-air museum in the same complex, is a spectacular example of 'green architecture'.

The land for the Boboli Gardens was bought by the Medici as a site for a new ducal palace and developed from the 15th to 19th Centuries. The Medici and Lorraine families enriched and expanded the gardens during the 17th to 19th Centuries, adding an outdoor museum.

As there was no natural water source, a conduit was built from the nearby River Arno to feed water into the Boboli complex irrigation system to encourage fertility, and to power various fountains by the amphitheatre in the garden.

Where different types of citrus trees are planted in close proximity, they cross-pollinate freely, adding to the diversity of the fruit. Mutations can be triggered by weather phenomena such as periods of drought or high rainfall, substantial temperature changes or strong winds. Given that some trees will have blossom and fruit on branches at the same time, this can result in fascinating attractive features to add to a citrus collection such as that at Boboli.

Sometimes deformed fruit are a result of mites. *Aceria Sheldoni* (citrus bud mite) attacks lemon blossom buds and damages flowers, resulting in digitated or fingered fruit. So unusual and collectable are some of the results that the mite, although a pest, has been called *acaro delle meraviglie*, or 'mite of the marvels'.

Digitated lemons and other strangely deformed fruits are known as *bizzarrie* in Italy. Paulo Galeotti, curator of the magnificent citrus collection at the Boboli Gardens in Florence, grafted a bizzarria that combined the physical properties of a sour orange with those of a citron and a lemon, to ensure that these strange fruit would not disappear.

Then there are citrus *chimeras* from the Greek for 'monster'. A chimera is a curious mutation where one or more carpels or segments in a fruit are very different from the rest of the fruit. Clearly a *monster* is not marketable. Much research is needed to determine what happens and why, given that many citrus fruit are mutations.

A fingered citron (*citrus medica var. sarcodactylis*) originally from China and North East India, produces fingered fruit naturally. With no flesh, it is just pith with a highly scented rind. Cultivated in China since the 10th Century, it is called *Buddha's Hand* and is used to scent clothes and rooms.

Next door to the Boboli Gardens, people came to La Specola wishing to see the extraordinary collection of odd specimens it housed, such as horrific reptiles, colourful birds and huge mammals. The museum was characterized by its emphasis on displaying strange, rare and foreign materials, and stressing their unusualness. The Medici's *Studiolo Collection*, which was abundant in precious specimens, was maintained largely intact.

The zoological exhibits housed in this eclectic museum consisted of many Italian and foreign specimens, and among them on display were several amazing animals, peculiar for their provenance, rarity or dimensions, which stirred the imagination of museum visitors.

There is a stuffed hippopotamus – possibly a 17th Century Medici pet – that once lived in the Boboli Gardens and was donated to the Grand Duke in the second half of the 18th Century.

A collection of mineralogical items with some of the world's largest crystals, as well as great educational materials on geology and palaeontology, are also found in this unusual museum.

La Specola is known for its vast collection of extremely life-like wax anatomical models from the 18th Century. Italian anatomists performed detailed dissections of human corpses that were then exactly reproduced with great precision as 3-D wax anatomical replicas.

These wax models served as illustrations for medical students studying at this scientific institute from the 1770s onwards. They were designed to help with the study of anatomy, while offering an alternative to dissection, and are beautiful reproductions of the human body in minute detail.

At the same time, a school was created in Florence to teach the art of making wax models. Today, the models form part of the extensive displays at La Specola and make up one of the world's most spectacular collections of its kind. Even now these exhibits are considered excellent reproductions with few anatomical errors

These bizarre wax anatomical models might be one reason why children in Florence eagerly drag their parents from one room to another in this museum. Vast, impressive, but eerie, the collection also encompasses pickled creepy-crawlies and stuffed specimens from every branch of the animal kingdom.

The museum has many diverse examples of extinct animals and a selection of taxidermy including hundreds of birds, insects and other organic samples. It houses over 3.5 million animal specimens, 5,000 of which are on display to the public.

La Specola is still a public museum, and with its numerous interesting botanical and zoological specimens and models, forms what must be the most unusual and spectacular legacy of the Medici empire.

Maintaining and conserving the La Specola collection requires great care as many exhibits are extremely fragile, and highly susceptible to temperature changes, moisture, strong light and vibrations caused by visitors walking around. As a result, the number of visitors is limited and visits need to be pre-booked.

Citrus forms an important part of the La Specola collection. Antique books and works of reference cover the history of the orchards and ornamental fruit, along with details of recently rediscovered plaster casts made in the 18th Century from the Medici citrus collection.

An assembly of 23 fragile citrus plaster casts, whose surface pigments have disintegrated over time, were found wrapped in rags and casually stored in bags and cardboard boxes. Even in their poor state, it was clear from these casts that the lemon was an ever-changing and variable part of the Medici citrus collection. Lemons with various split skins or fruit within fruit, took their place beside distorted mutants and dull citrus monsters.

These citrus casts were stored at the Boboli Gardens. A few of them have been restored, but the rest appear to have been abandoned for the time being.

In complete contrast to the dusty plaster casts, the Botany Department of the Officina di Ceroplastica contains wax models that were originally displayed alongside the casts in La Specola. There are models of oranges, lemons and citrons made in wax from the plaster casts taken originally from real fruit in the Boboli Gardens.

These wax models, with the luminosity of real citrus fruit, are displayed in glass cases. They are hardly beautiful, given that they show the distortions and misshapen fruit, but they are certainly a magnificent record of Mother Nature at her most diverse.

While modern citrus grove trees may live for 40 or more years, there are some historical examples of citrus trees in Italy and Spain that have lived for several hundred years. The Boboli Gardens, Villa de Piedra and Garden of Villa Medici at Castello in Florence all have *Liminaia* ('lemon houses'), or homes to protect citrus plants from winter frosts and ensure their long life.

Built in the 18th Century, these Liminaia protect some of Europe's most important collections of rare and exotic citrus plants during the cold winter months. Some of the distorted, asymmetrical citrus trees, with their gnarled rootstocks and split branches, are at least 300 years old. In particular, the trees at Castello were grafted onto sour orange rootstock, the only kind of citrus hardy enough to survive the winter cold in Florence, and this explains their longevity.

Through a lack of effective maintenance, the structure of the Limonaia at the Boboli Gardens progressively decayed and became extremely fragile. But fortunately, it was included in the 1998 World Monuments Watch (WMF).

Beginning in 2001, the WMF assisted the local authorities with the restoration of the roof and façade of the Limonaia. Through extensive documentation and laser scanning, the condition of the façade was mapped and treatment proposals were prepared. This study revealed an alteration to the surface along a vertical crack hidden under a layer of plaster on the façade, which confirmed an extension of the building.

Following this discovery, the surfaces of the structure were cleaned and its cracks repaired. Traditional lime putty and sand mortars were used for the integration of missing parts. Broken stained glass windows were replaced with new glass from Germany.

The Limonaia is now an important feature of the Boboli Gardens, and its restoration allows visitors to have an even richer experience in appreciating the grandeur of the grounds envisioned by the Medici for the area surrounding the Palazzo Pitti, and Boboli Gardens complex itself.

ORANGERIES

Around the end of the 15th Century, Charles VIII of France went to Italy with the aim of calming the peninsula's unrest by force, but instead, he fell in love with Italian art, architecture and oranges. When he returned to France, he brought with him Italian gardeners, architects and artists to transform the castles and gardens of France. He also built the first orangery at his château at Amboise.

At that time citrus trees in northern Europe were a sign of wealth, and an orangery was a major status symbol. For the next 200 years orangeries became *de rigueur* in French palaces. The citrus trees were often planted in vast, highly porous terracotta pots which provided ideal conditions for citrus as they can't tolerate being waterlogged. Other trees were planted in giant wooden boxes and moved in and outdoors depending on the weather. Some boxes had wheels, making them easy to move.

Royal orangeries started appearing across northern Europe, competing for size and status.

Louis XIV wanted an orangery at Versailles that reflected the image of absolute monarchy, by showcasing the skills of the 17th Century's greatest French artists and scientists. The Versailles Orangery took nearly 10 years to build but was the talk and envy of the entire aristocratic world, and became the venue for majestic garden parties, banquets and balls.

But nothing would compare with the pretensions of the orangery in Dresden called the Zwinger. It was built in the early 18th Century by Frederick Augustus I, Elector of Saxony. He intended it to be the size of the palace, but he ran out of money.

The German town of Oranienbaum, which has a bronze orange tree in the marketplace symbolizing the House of Orange, also boasts one of the longest orangeries in Europe.

CITRUS IN TUDOR AND STUART TIMES

Citrus fruits were expensive and therefore limited to the wealthy in Tudor times. In Elizabethan England sweetmeats at court included candied orange peel made with rose water and sugar.

The battle of Lepanto on 7th October 1571 was a remarkable naval victory in which the Spanish Empire inflicted a major defeat on the Ottoman Empire in the Gulf of Patras, and effectively marked the turning point of the Ottoman Empire's expansion in the Mediterranean. Tudor chicken with orange sauce was a popular dish for nobility created at the time to commemorate this achievement.

In Tudor times, a few oranges were grown in southern England, but found the climate difficult. The famous Elizabethan courtier, Sir Walter Raleigh (1552–1618) planted oranges seeds in Surrey, and the trees began bearing regular crops in 1595. Covered to protect them from the cold in winter, they survived for 178 years, but were killed by the bitter winter of 1739–40.

HOUSE OF ORANGE

The name of the House of Orange is an example of the use of the word *orange* without any direct link to orange trees or fruit. Instead, this dynasty derived its name from the medieval Principality of Orange, a city in old Provence, southern France. This princely dynasty was important in the history of the Netherlands and today provides that nation's royal family.

The House of Orange-Nassau was established as a result of the marriage of Henry III of Nassau-Breda from Germany and Claudia of Châlon-Orange from French Burgundy in 1515. Henry and Claudia had a son, René.

Claudia's brother was Philibert of Châlon (1502–1530), the Prince of Orange, who was awarded a substantial part of the Netherlands for his political and military services to the Holy Roman Emperor, Charles V. Since Philibert had no immediate heir, when he was killed at the age of 28, in the final stages of the siege of Florence in 1530, René, inherited the independent and sovereign Principality of Orange from Philibert.

As the first Nassau to be the Prince of Orange, René could have used Orange-Nassau as his new family name. However, his uncle had stipulated in his will that René should continue the use of the name Châlon-Orange. History, therefore, knows him as René of Châlon.

After René's premature death in battle in 1544, his cousin, William of Nassau-Dillenburg, brought up as a Lutheran, inherited all his lands in the low countries (today the Netherlands and Belgium) and all his titles, including Prince of Orange, on condition he received a Roman Catholic education. He also inherited the Principality of Orange (in today's France) and significant lands in Germany. This William I of Orange, who was better known in England as William the Silent, (1533–1584) became the founder of the House of Orange-Nassau and the Dutch Republic.

William the Silent married four times and his fourth wife, Louise de Coligny, a French Huguenot, was the mother of Frederik Hendrik (1584–1647), William's fourth legitimate son.

While living in Germany, William the Silent ignored the summons of Fernando Álvarez de Toledo y Pimental, (known in Spain as the Grand Duke of Alva and in the Netherlands as the Iron Duke) to return to Brussels. He remained in Germany, with the result that his first son, Philip William, only a boy of 13, was kidnapped as a hostage in 1568 and taken to Spain to be brought up as a Catholic. Philip William did not see his father again.

On the death of William the Silent in 1584, Philip William succeeded him as the Prince of Orange, but remained in Spain, only returning to the Netherlands in 1596. Philip William died in Brussels in 1618, to be succeeded by his half brother, Maurice, from William the Silent's second marriage.

As Prince of Orange, Maurice, a strong military leader, won several victories over the Spanish, but died in 1625 from liver disease. As there was no legitimate heir, Frederik Hendrik, Maurice's half-brother (and William the Silent's youngest son by his fourth marriage) inherited the title of Prince of Orange.

Frederik Hendrik died in 1647 and was succeeded by his only son, William II as the Prince of Orange, who also succeeded his father as Stadtholder, that is, the chief magistrate of the United Provinces of the Netherlands.

In 1641, Prince William II of Orange-Nassau married the blue-blooded Mary Stuart, daughter of the English King, Charles I. However, this close relationship with the royal Stuart family represented a potential threat to the liberty of the Netherlands.

At the time of William II's marriage to his then 19-year-old bride, the throne of her father, Charles I, was already in danger.

In 1642, civil war broke out in England between the royalists and the Parliament. Charles I was beheaded in 1649 and England became the Republican Commonwealth of England and Ireland with Oliver Cromwell as head of state. Cromwell was known as the Lord Protector of England, Scotland, and Ireland from 1653 to 1658.

Although William II wanted to come to the assistance of the Stuarts, he did not receive any support from the government. He was also at variance with the States of Holland. They wanted to lay off troops on a large scale following the Treaty of Munster, whereas William II wanted nothing better than to resume the war with Spain.

William II took up arms and sent his cousin to seize Amsterdam. Talks were held, but the prince died unexpectedly of smallpox on 6th November 1650 at the age of 24. The States decided that no new Stadtholder would be appointed for the time being, thus marking the beginning of the First Stadtholderless Period (1651–1672).

A son, William, was born to William II of Orange and his wife, Mary of England, in The Hague one week after his father's death in November 1650.

A protestant prince of the House of Orange and powerful leader, William III was a grandson of Charles I. He became William III, King of England, Scotland and Ireland from 1689-1702, and married Mary II of England, daughter of the English King, James II, in 1677, but died childless.

THE ORANGE ORDER

In the 17th Century, predominantly Catholic Ireland was viewed as brutal and uncivilised. The King of England was the Lord of Ireland – a title granted by the Pope back in the 12th Century. However, religion remained a contentious issue in Ireland between the Catholic majority and the Protestant minority.

In the war between Philip II of Spain and Elizabeth I of England, the Spaniards viewed Ireland as a back door into England. Later the French also saw Ireland as a vulnerable way into England. Even in the 20th Century in World War I, Germany thought the same.

The period 1536–1691 saw the first full conquest and colonisation of Ireland by England with Protestant settlers from Great Britain. This led to Ireland being subordinated to a London-based government along with sectarian animosity between Catholics and Protestants. Henry VIII, who reigned from 1509–47, claimed to be King of Catholic Ireland, but he was a Protestant and had fallen out with the Pope. And the impact on England of this Irish "weak spot" in the late 1600s made the British governors of Ireland extremely worried about this insecurity.

As they mainly remained Catholic, the Irish looked for allies in other European Catholic countries such as Spain and France, so their political centre of gravity moved away from England.

Spain saw this as an opportunity, and in 1601 sent a fleet of 28 ships to occupy the Irish port of Kinsale, but this was unsuccessful when they were besieged by English forces.

The Irish had long resented the English since their conquest of Ireland in the 16th Century. The Nine Year's War, a rebellion against the English centred in the north of Ireland, ended in 1603 when the Gallic leaders made peace with the Treaty of Mellifont. But both the Irish and the English continued to harbour grievances over land and religion.

With the policy of the Plantation of Ulster, which had started in 1606, settlers moved from England and Scotland, staking claims to plots of land in Ulster and seizing the opportunity to colonise and tame the landscape to the disadvantage of the indigenous Irish. The Plantation policy was seen as a way to control, anglicise and civilise Ulster, and it continued until 1641.

Scotland experienced a catastrophic famine for seven years in the 1690s, with failed harvests and dire food shortages – called the Lean Years. This led to a further wave of Scots moving to Ireland, many of whom were hardened by Scottish Calvinism and imbued with a strong sense of self-sufficiency, and a "no surrender" ethic. They regarded themselves as a Protestant garrison of the British State, protecting mainland Britain by establishing a frontier zone across the Irish Sea.

As James II, James (1633-1701) was King of England and Ireland, and as James VII, he was King of Scotland until he was deposed in the Glorious Revolution of 1688. James converted to Catholicism in 1670, although his two daughters were raised as Protestants, and he became hugely unpopular because of his persecution of the Protestant clergy.

When James was overthrown in 1688, he fled to France. He was replaced by his Protestant daughter, Mary II, who acceded to the Crowns of England and Scotland and reigned jointly with her Dutch Protestant husband (also her cousin), William of Orange (William III).

James II plotted to regain his throne, and landed in Ireland in 1689, but his attempt was thwarted in 1690 when the Battle of the Boyne took place across the River Boyne near the town of Drogheda, 30 miles north of Dublin in the then Kingdom of Ireland.

This battle was between the forces of the deposed King James II/VII, and those of the Dutch Prince William of Orange, (William III) who was sometimes known in Northern Ireland as King Billy.

With infantry from the Netherlands, Denmark and the Huguenots, William of Orange secured victory. After James II's failed attempt to regain the British Crown, he returned to exile in France, and ultimately the continuing Protestant Ascendancy in Ireland was aided.

The symbolic importance of the Battle of the Boyne has made it one of the best-known battles in the history of the British Isles and a key part of the folklore of the Protestant Orange Order.

Religion has long been a source of tension in Ireland. In 1795 supporters of William of Orange founded the Loyal Orange Institution, or the Orange Order, after a stand-off in County Armagh, known as the Battle of the Diamond, between the Roman Catholic Defenders and the Protestants Peep O'Day Boys.

The order's name comes from the House of Orange and the Protestant King William of Orange who had defeated Catholic King James at the Battle of the Boyne in July 1690. The Orange Society was a Masonic-style fraternity sworn to maintain the Protestant Ascendancy, with the first commemorative parades being held in 1796.

Today the society is headed by the Grand Orange Lodge of Ireland. Its name remains a tribute to the Dutch-born protestant King William of Orange. Its members wear orange sashes and are referred to as Orangemen.

Although the *Orange* in the Orange Order has no direct link with the citrus fruit, the influence of the Battle of the Boyne and the formation of the Orange Order still has considerable resonance in British history. The Order continues to hold passionate yearly marches commemorating the Battle of the Boyne, with Orange Men marching through the streets of Northern Ireland each year on the 12th of July.

ORANGE WORLDWIDE

The House of Orange led directly to the word 'orange' having a number of global applications, and it has found its way into a number of other fields.

THE ORANGE RIVER

The Orange River, named in honour of the Dutch ruling family by the Dutch explorer Robert Jacob Gordon, is the longest river in South Africa. Rising in the Drakensberg Mountains in Lesotho, it meanders westwards through South Africa. The river basin extends into Botswana to the north and forms part of the international border with Namibia as it goes west to the Atlantic Ocean.

FORT ORANGE

The present-day city of Albany, New York State, was originally named Fort Orange and was the first permanent Dutch settlement in New Netherlands. It was built in 1624 as a replacement for Fort Nassau, which had previously been on nearby Castle Island and served as a trading post until 1617, when it was abandoned due to frequent flooding. Both forts were named in honour of the Dutch House of Orange-Nassau.

THE ORANGE FREE STATE

The Orange Free State was an independent Boer sovereign republic founded in 1854 in Southern Africa. The capital was Bloemfontein and the common language was Dutch, with a second language of Afrikaans. It ceased to exist after it was defeated and surrendered to the British Empire at the end of the Second Boer War in 1902. The name was changed to the Orange River Colony, then in 1910 it became one of the provinces of the new Union of South Africa, and its name changed back to the Orange Free State.

CAPE ORANGE

Dutch explorers called the northernmost point of the Brazilian coastline and State of Amapá, South America, Cape Orange. This tidal marshland is now part of the Cabo Orange National Park. It is known as the only place on the Brazilian coast where the American flamingo nests.

CROWN DUCAL ORANGE TREE TABLEWARE

A G Richardson & Co Ltd, founded in 1915 and based in Tunstall, Staffordshire, was a successful manufacturer of porcelain and high-grade earthenware in the 1920s and 1930s. Using the trade name Crown Ducal Ware, their china designs were strongly influenced by the art deco movement (1905–1935).

In 1925 Richardson launched Pattern Number A1211, known as 'Orange Tree', which was to become one of their most memorable ranges. Created by renowned art deco designer Norman Keates, this pattern features black trees and trim, with orange fruit.

Alternative names for this design are 'Woodlands' and 'Pomegranate' but it is best known as 'Orange Tree'.

ORANGE MOBILE NETWORK

Orange UK was a mobile network operator and internet service provider in the United Kingdom. It was founded in 1993 and launched to customers on 28th April 1994. It was once in the FTSE 100 Index but was purchased by France Télécom (now Orange S.A.) in 2000, which then adopted the Orange brand for all its other mobile communications activities. Orange UK merged with Deutsche Telekom's T-Mobile UK to form a joint venture, EE in 2010. EE continued to operate the Orange brand until February 2015, when new connections and upgrades on Orange tariffs were withdrawn. Existing Orange customers could remain on their plans until March 2019.

PLAZA DE LOS NARANJOS

If visiting Marbella, Spain, be sure to check out the Plaza de los Naranjos (Orange Square) one of the liveliest areas in the heart of the Old Town. At the end of the 15th Century, having re-conquered the city of Marbella from the Moors, the Christian authorities decided to follow the trend of other Spanish towns, and in 1485 they demolished some of the whitewashed structures to make way for a pleasant open space where residents could gather to socialise. Thus Marbella's Plaza de los Naranjos was born.

A selection of traditional Castilian Renaissance architecture forms the backdrop to a variety of open-air cafés and restaurants. Here is the Town Hall, the eye-catching Casa del Corregidor, or Mayor's House, with its Gothic façade, and a statue of King Juan Carlos I. And don't miss the Chapel de Santiago, the oldest religious building in Marbella. Sit and relax with a coffee or glass of wine, while breathing in the sweet scent of the orange blossom from the many citrus trees.

CITRUS MUSEUMS

Built in 1935, and now listed on the National Register of Historic Places, the Heritage Center and Indian River Citrus Museum provide a glimpse into the past of Vero Beach, Florida. Here you can discover why Indian River citrus fruit is so special. For more details, see Appendix B.

The city of Burriana, in Castellon, north of the heart of the fertile Valencian orange groves on Spain's Costa del Azahar is believed to have had the only Museum in Europe devoted to oranges and other citrus fruit, but unfortunately it is no longer open.

RATIONED ORANGE JUICE

During and after World War II, UK children had their own ration books. To supplement wartime food rations, the Ministry of Food introduced fruit juice in the autumn of 1941. Initially, it was mainly blackcurrant or rose-hip juice, but by 1943, with increased supplies available under Lend-Lease, sweetened concentrated welfare orange juice was offered to children from the age of six months up to five years old. The aim was to give young children a source of Vitamin C at a time when few fresh oranges were available in the shops, thus helping to protect them from scurvy and other similar illnesses.

Welfare foods have never been fully taken up by the public, but by 1948 36 per cent of those entitled to do so took advantage of this freely available juice. It didn't taste like fresh orange juice but it did have a distinctive syrupy tang that was quite palatable.

Rationing ceased in July 1954, with much of the State juice coming from oranges grown and processed in the British West Indies in the latter years.

BATTLE OF THE ORANGES

In Ivrea, northern Italy, a three-day Battle of the Oranges takes place each year on the Sunday, Monday and Tuesday ending on the night of Shrove Tuesday.

People are asked to wear a special red hat, the *berretta frigio*, or else they can be considered a "fair target for gentle and moderate orange throwing".

The red hat is a symbol of freedom that was worn in Roman times by freed slaves, and during the Middle Ages it was on the heads of peasants rioting against feudal lords.

Teams of *aranceri* or 'orange throwers' on foot, wearing uniforms, hurl oranges at their opponents on horse-drawn carriages, clad in "Doctor Whoesque" costumes with padded shoulders and leather-covered cylindrical helmets.

The carnival is the celebration of a medieval rebellion. Feudal lords had the right to sleep with brides on their first wedding night. In 1194, the beautiful miller Violetta promised her fiancé she would refuse to subdue. Alone with the lord in his chamber, Violetta drew a dagger and beheaded him, then showed the head to the people standing around the castle walls.

This event sparked a revolt. The castle was set on fire and the people marched victorious, led by their heroine.

During current Battles of the Oranges, the *aranceri* on foot represent the people, the lord's army are those in the horse-drawn carriages, whose protections are supposed to be reminiscent of Medieval armour.

Today it is an opportunity for Italians to re-live the historical war that broke out between nobility and peasants in a relatively harmless way, even if there are a fair number of black eyes and bruises at the end of the festival.

LEMONADE SAVED PARIS

The refreshing and natural drink of lemonade is easily made with lemon juice, sugar or honey, and iced water.

Lemonade would appear to have been around for centuries and was possibly invented in ancient Egypt. However, much later it had a great impact on Paris, where it became a popular drink in the 17th Century, with pavement café owners known as *limonadiers*.

In 1665, many European cities were stricken by the Great Plague, the worst outbreak of bubonic plague since the Black Death of 1348. London lost roughly 25 per cent of its population, with more than seven thousand Londoners dying in one week at its peak, while the French capital was largely spared.

With no sanitation in 17th Century cities, rubbish was alive with rats. At this time a drop in the price of West Indian sugar and the availability of lemons from Italy led to an increase in the consumption of lemonade which became a favourite thirst-quencher in Paris. The discarded lemon peels that were tossed in the streets contained limonene and linalool, two chemicals that act as pest repellents.

At the time they did not know why Paris escaped, but years later it was discovered that the plague was carried from rats to humans by infected fleas. Chemicals in the discarded lemon peel killed the fleas, thus helping to protect the Parisian inhabitants.

Today both limonene and linalool are found in pet shampoos and sprays used for killing both adult fleas and their eggs.

HISTORICAL AND LITERARY REFERENCES

References to oranges and other citrus in history and classical literature abound.

Cardinal Thomas Wolsey (1473–1530) was renowned for carrying around a scented orange saturated in vinegar to insulate him from the noxious airs of London and his fellow men.

By the 16th Century oranges and lemons were prized across Europe both for their flavour and their perfume. Noblemen and women carried delicate silver filigreed containers holding orange peel to mask the rank odours of the street.

Shakespeare has many references to citrus. In *Love's Labours Lost* (1598), for instance, one character proclaims: "The armipotent Mars, of lances the almighty, Gave Hector a gift …," to which another puckishly suggests: "A lemon."

Then in *Hamlet* Act 1 Scene 5 Shakespeare mentions the citrus dessert posset and its medicinal properties:

"And with sudden vigour it doth posset,
And curd, like aigre [sour] droppings into milk,
The thin and wholesome blood."

Shakespeare also cites posset eaten for pleasure in *The Merry Wives of Windsor*, Act 5, Scene 5:

"Yet be cheerful knight: thou shalt eat a posset tonight at my house;
Where I will desire thee to laugh at my wife."

According to Elizabeth David in her book *I'll be with you in the squeezing of a lemon*:

"In 1533 the Company of Leathersellers offered Henry the Eighth and Anne Boleyn a great banquet to celebrate Anne's coronation on Whit Sunday in Westminster Hall. Among the princely luxuries which graced the feast was one lemon, one only, for which the Leathersellers had paid six silver pennies."

Diarist Samuel Pepys (1633–1703) on 9th March 1669 had his first glass of orange juice and wrote: "I drank a glass, of a pint, I believe, at one drought, of the juice of oranges, of whose peel they make comfits, and here they drink the juice as wine, with sugar, and it is a very fine drink, but it being new, I was doubtful whether it might not do me hurt".

During the Restoration, young women carried baskets of oranges and stood near the stage of London theatres, facing the audience and selling oranges at sixpence apiece, and themselves for a little more. These orange girls worked under the control of women called the Orange Molls. Nell Gwyn, a beautiful and illiterate orange girl, became a minor actress and the mistress of King Charles II. Nell died when she was 37, but she had lived to see her son made Duke of St Albans.

The influence of *orange* has even been applied to potentially trivial topics. Carrots were originally a dark mauve, yellow or white in colour. In the 17th Century, the Dutch developed a strain that contained higher levels of beta carotene and so became the orange colour they are today. This was designed to please the royal family of the House of Orange.

There are many examples in literature of references to citrus fruit. One appears in Flora Thompson's *Lark Rise to Candleford* which talks of oranges with a strange foreign scent and "orange pith dried on the hob and taken to school as a type of chewing gum."

Later there's mention that: "The first to arrive on Monday morning was old Jerry Parish with his cartload of fish and fruit . . . he took round to the doors at Lark Rise a box of bloaters and a basket of small, sour oranges. The bloaters were sold at a penny each and the oranges at three a penny. Even at these prices they were luxuries."

I ORANGE JUICING MACHINE

Customers can make their own fresh juice in Spanish supermarkets

II LEMON HOUSE
Citrus plants in Florence are taken indoors during winter to protect them from the frosts

III LEMON HOUSE
Some Florence citrus trees are very old or obscure mutants, so they need to be protected from winter frosts in a lemon house. Florence has several of these old Limonaia.

IV BOTTICELLI'S *PRIMAVERA*

Botticelli's Primavera (Spring) shows a group of figures in an orange grove, with Mercury on the left reaching up into the orange trees, chasing away the clouds of winter and welcoming spring

V BOTTICELLI'S *PRIMAVERA*

Close up of Mercury among the orange trees

VI FERDINAND AND ISABELLA

Statue of the Spanish Catholic Kings, Ferdinand and Isabella, who funded Christopher Columbus and his journeys to the New World

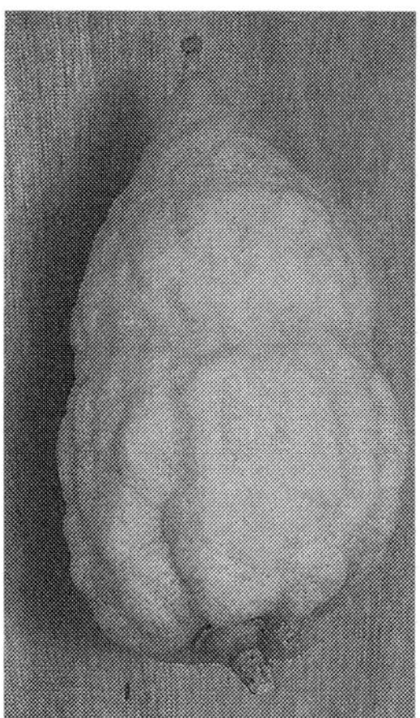

VII ETROG

An Israeli etrog, with pitam and gartel (ridge around the centre) Photo attribution: יעקב [CC BY-SA 3.0 (https://creativecommons.org/licenses/by-sa/3.0)]

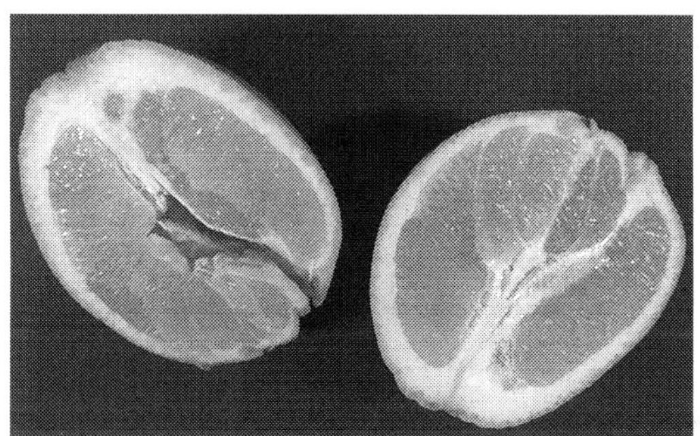

VIII CUT NAVEL ORANGE

Showing a 'baby' orange inside the main orange

IX SATSUMA WITH A 'BABY' INSIDE

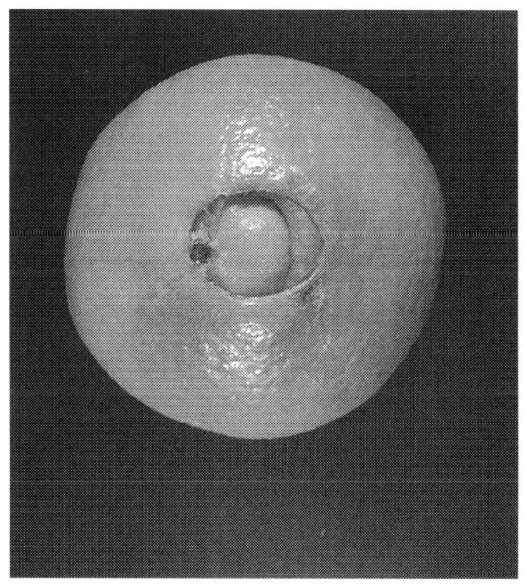

X DISTINCTIVE BASE OF NAVEL ORANGE

XI FINGER LIMES
(Photo courtesy of Fine Food Specialist) For their full range of products, go to: https://www.finefoodspecialist.co.uk/

XII FINGER LIME, SPILLING OUT ITS JUICE VESICLES
(Photo courtesy of Plants4Presents) For details of their range of plants, visit https://plants4presents.co.uk/

XIII YUZU FRUIT
(Photo courtesy of Plants4Presents)
For details of their range of plants, visit https://plants4presents.co.uk/

XIV KUMQUATS
(Photo courtesy of Fine Food Specialist)
For their full range of products, go to: https://www.finefoodspecialist.co.uk/

XV BLOOD ORANGES

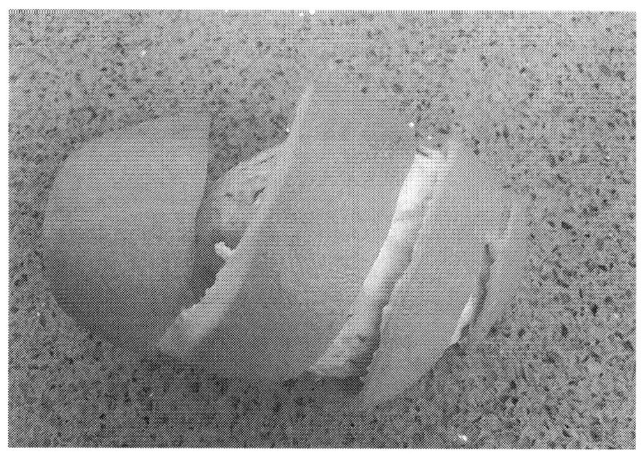

XVI ORANGE PEELED AS A SPIRAL IN ONE PIECE

XVII PEELED ORANGE WITH RUBBER BAND

The complete spiral of peel is held in place over the fruit by a rubber band, making it easy to add to a packed lunch

XVIII INDIAN RIVER CITRUS MUSEUM
(Photo courtesy Vero Heritage Indian River Citrus Museum – photography by Steve Erickson) Further details from https://www.veroheritage.org/

XIX INDIAN RIVER CITRUS MUSEUM
Close up of some exhibits
(Photo courtesy Vero Heritage Indian River Citrus Museum – photography by Steve Erickson) Further details from https://www.veroheritage.org/

XX CHINOTTO TREE
Makes a good house plant, with plenty of fruit
(Photo courtesy of Plants4Presents) For details of their range of plants, visit https://plants4presents.co.uk/

XXI CHINOTTO FRUIT
(Photo courtesy of Plants4Presents) For details of their range of plants, visit https://plants4presents.co.uk/

XXII POMELO
This large fruit is 6-10 inches in diameter

XXIII VERNA LEMONS
One of the most popular types of lemon

Chapter 3.

TYPES OF CITRUS FRUIT

In the 21st Century, the orange is one of the most commonly cultivated fruit trees across the world though it is only relatively recently that oranges have been eaten as food. Previously, they were used for the ornamental appearance of the trees and the inspiring aroma of their blossom and peel. They also provided seasoning for fish and meat but were rarely consumed whole.

Some of the most popular varieties of citrus fruits include sweet oranges, sour oranges, blood oranges, mandarins, lemons, limes and grapefruit.

According to the website of the University of California Riverside, College of Natural and Agricultural Sciences, Citrus Variety Collections, there are well over 1,100 different citrus varieties, each with its own description.
(Website: https://citrusvariety.ucr.edu/)

Given the vast range of hybrids, cross-pollination and other cultivars, it is hardly surprising that some develop 'sports', or parts of the plant that show morphological (ie structural) differences from the main part of the plant, which can be by foliage shape or colour, flowers, fruit or branch structure.

Among the hundreds of different species of citrus fruit, some have been created intentionally, with others by chance or accident. Only a relatively small number of varieties are commercially viable.

A selection of key species is discussed below, and more details of individual fruits are included in the Table of Citrus Fruit in Appendix A.

SWEET ORANGES

Sweet oranges are used to produce juice or peel and are also eaten whole. They have tight skins, reproduce asexually, and many, but not all varieties, are larger than mandarins.

An evergreen sweet orange tree will grow anything from 5–10+ metres (16–33+ feet) high, although some may be kept small for easy harvesting. Individual oranges are usually round or elliptical, with a diameter of 7–10 cm (3–4 inches).

Oranges with five or fewer seeds are said to be seedless, although some people who buy them as *seedless* may complain when they find the odd seed.

VALENCIAS

Valencias (*Citrus sinensis*) are the main type of orange used for eating as fruit and for making orange juice. They are delicious, very juicy and regarded as seedless, although they may have the occasional seed. They are large, round and have a thick skin and are one of the most popular varieties cultivated extensively worldwide.

Unlike many other orange trees, Valencias are in bloom and fruit at the same time, with the current year's oranges interspersed among the flowers for the next year's crop.

NAVELS

Navel (*Citrus sinensis*) oranges are the most common variety of orange that is eaten. They are also good to juice but the juice tends to be so sweet that it ferments easily. Consequently, if fresh, it needs to be used within a few hours, or it will become bitter. Alternatively, it can be pasteurised. Navels are seedless and are in season from November into June in the Northern Hemisphere.

They have comparatively thick skins, and on the end where the blossom was, have a characteristic navel-like mark resembling a mini orange. As a result, navels are seen to imitate a degree of fertility as they seek to reproduce a fruit within a fruit.

OLD NAVELS

There are many varieties of navel orange, some of which are very old. Navels were seen as the fruit of the Gods – they might have been the *Golden Apples* of the Garden of Hesperides which were stolen by Hercules.

Both ancient Greeks and Romans tended to call all fruit *apples*, thus causing some confusion. In later years, it was thought that the *Golden Apples* might actually have been oranges, a fruit hardly known in Europe and the Mediterranean before the Middle Ages.

Some historic navel trees have produced as many as 12,000 oranges, but the average yield per tree is closer to 1,500.

Many currently grown strains of navels originated in Bahia, Brazil, possibly as a mutation of the Brazilian Selecta Orange. There is some dispute as to how this orange made its way to California.

One story has it that in 1870 an American Presbyterian missionary visiting Brazil was impressed by the seedlessness and rich flavour of this unusual winter orange with an umbilicus at its blossom end.

A dozen of these navel trees were sent to the Department of Agriculture in Washington, DC, where they were propagated under glass. Offered to anyone who wanted to try them out, they became known as Washington Navels.

Mrs Luther C Tibbets of Riverside, California requested a pair of these trees which she successfully planted. Locals admired the fruit and news spread to the rest of the world, with many of today's navels having descended from these trees, with numerous variations.

The Californian Carter navel is thin skinned, very sweet and the trees bear abundant crops. Like the Washington navel, the Carter matures slightly earlier and its flavour is somewhat sweeter.

The Robertson Navel is virtually indistinguishable from the Washington, except again it matures slightly earlier. Although it is heat resistant and prolific, its tree lacks vigour, so it is not commercially important. However, because of its small tree size, it is popular as a container-grown patio tree.

The Thomson is yet another variety of navel with a thinner, smoother rind. It is less well coloured than the Washington navel, with a slightly elongated shape, but also matures somewhat earlier than the Washington.

JAFFAS®

In the Middle East, cultivation of oranges in the region surrounding the city of Jaffa, Israel, began during the Ottoman period in the 19th Century, as a result of trade with the Far East. The moderate climate and fertile soil proved to be ideal conditions for citrus growing, giving rise to the then famous Shamouti orange.

The sweet Shamouti orange is almost seedless and has a fine, succulent flavour. Its deep orange-coloured, thick, leathery skin peels easily. These oranges were grown in Hadera, Gaza, Tiberias, Jericho, the Jordan Valley and Jaffa. With thousands of orchards surrounding the city, Jaffa was the only port to export citrus from the late 19th Century until the establishment of modern ports in Tel Aviv, Haifa and Ashdod, so they became known as Jaffa® Oranges (*Citrus sinensis* Jaffa®).

Today, Jaffa® has become a generic name for high-quality citrus fruit. Over the past 70 years, the Jaffa® brand has evolved to cover a variety of citrus fruits, including oranges, mandarins, grapefruit and lemons, in addition to multiple other hybrids and cultivars. Israeli producers have sold shamouti budwood to Spanish growers who can now use the Jaffa® name, which is an Israeli trademark.

KUMQUATS

Kumquats (*Citrus japonica*) are the smallest commercially available oranges. These little yellow citrus fruits are a bit sour but have edible peels. They are eaten whole with the peel being the sweetest part of the fruit. Often called the *golden orange* they are often used for decorating, and the pulp of the fruit is preserved.

Candied kumquats can be the highlight on the table at Chinese New Year and are sometimes part of pork dishes. Although vanilla is not naturally found in Chinese cooking, the best candied kumquats have both vanilla and cinnamon added. Kumquats can also be crystallized or preserved in honey, occasionally with salt added.

MALTAISE SANGUINE

Sometimes referred to as the 'Queen of Oranges' the Maltaise Sanguine (*Citrus sinensis* (L.) Osbeck) is a slightly pigmented orange with a sublime flavour, soft, juicy, melting segments, and a wonderful blend of sweetness with just the right, tangy acidity. The skin is relatively thick but easy to peel, and is slightly pebbled with a deep orange colour and a hint of pigmentation. The fruit is relatively small for an orange and it is harvested in March and April.

The Maltaise Sanguine comes from Tunisia but is rarely seen in England as most are exported to France where it is highly prized.

SOUR ORANGES

Seville Oranges (*Citrus aurantium*), Bigarade or bitter oranges were originally native to Southeast Asia. They have spread to many parts of the world and today large numbers are cultivated in Spain following their introduction by the Moors at the beginning of the 10th Century. Some bitter orange trees in Spain are said to be over 600 years old.

The bitter orange has a thick, dimpled skin, and is believed to be a cross between *Citrus maxima* and *Citrus reticulata*. This tart orange is used to make marmalade and is now quite widely grown across the Mediterranean.

Sauce Bigarade is a classic French sauce for duck, *Bigarade* being the Provençal name for 'bitter orange'. It is a thickened stock flavoured with the rind of bitter orange, often with lemon juice and sugar added.

Sour oranges in Afghanistan are used as seasoning agents and squeezed over local dishes to cut the grease.

Sour orange rootstock is fairly tolerant of cold winter temperatures and poorly drained soils in comparison with other available rootstocks. Sour orange also produces a good tasting piece of fruit, but it can be subject to virus attacks.

Relatives of the bitter orange include the Bizzarria, (*citrus medica* + C. *aurantium*) a bi-coloured intermingling or grafted 'chimera' of bitter orange and either lemon or citron. There is also the Bouquetier de Nice (*Citrus aurantium*) which is used in neroli oils and perfumes, and Canaliculata or Striata (*Citrus aurantium*), a bittersweet orange with an unusual fruit. Its flesh is often sweet when ripe but the pith is bitter. The skin is ribbed in this ancient variety and is seen in some of the old Italian citrus paintings from around Leonardo da Vinci's time.

The Bergamot orange (*Citrus bergamia*) is a highly fragrant yellow/green fruit probably a hybrid of lemon and bitter orange. Extract of Bergamot is used in food, perfume and cosmetics, and to scent Earl Grey tea.

BLOOD ORANGES

The blood orange is a natural mutation of the sweet orange, with crimson streaks, and sometimes fabulous, almost blood-red coloured flesh. It is highly prized for eating throughout Europe.

The Arancia Rossa di Sicilia (red orange of Sicily) (*Citrus sinensis* 'Blood Orange') is a selection of fresh citrus fruit encompassing the Tarocco, Moro and Sanguinello blood orange varieties. With Protected Geographical Status, Arancia Rossa di Sicilia is produced in the provinces of Enna, Catania and Syracuse in Sicily.

Blood oranges are usually smaller than many other oranges. Their skin may or may not have a hint of red blush or splashes of rose on their otherwise orange peel. They are quite sweet and best used as fruit rather than for juice.

The red colour is due to the presences of anthocyanins, a family of antioxidant pigments common in many flowers and fruit. The red flesh develops when the fruit encounters low temperatures at night. Sometimes dark colouring is seen on the exterior of the rind as well as in the flesh, depending on the type of blood orange.

The skin is thin and may be tight or delicate. Some varieties can be hard to peel. Blood oranges have a unique flavour when compared with other oranges, having distinctly raspberry-like notes in addition to the usual citrus.

The three main types of blood orange are the Tarocco (native to Italy) the Sanguinello (native to Spain) and the Moro (native to Sicily), which is the newest of the three varieties.

TAROCCO

The Tarocco (*Citrus sinensis*) is one of the most popular oranges because of its raspberry rich sweetness and is possibly the strongest flavoured blood orange. Medium-sized, it has the highest Vitamin C content of any orange, mainly as a result of growing in the fertile soil around Mount Etna. Its orange skin has slight red blushes; it is seedless and easy to peel.

SANGUINELLO

The Sanguinello (*Citrus sinensis* (L.) 'Osbeck') blood orange was discovered in Spain in 1929. It had a clear yellow compact rind with a reddish tinge, few seeds and a sweet, tender, orange flesh with multiple blood-coloured streaks. It matures in February, but it can remain on the tree until April, so extending the harvest period.

MORO

Moro (*Citrus sinensis* 'Blood Orange') is the most colourful of the blood oranges. With deep red flesh that ranges from orange-veined with ruby colouration, to vermilion, vivid crimson, and sometimes even nearly black, and with a bright red blush to the peel, this orange certainly makes a statement. The Moro's somewhat bitter taste has raspberry overtones, with a flavour varying from that of a ripe cherry through to a passion fruit.

Blood oranges are expensive in comparison with mass-produced oranges, not just because they can be delicate, but partly because their season is quite short.

MANDARINS

The mandarin group includes mandarins, satsumas, clementines, tangerines, tangelos and tangors. All mandarins have a 'zipper' peel, a skin that grows around the segments of the fruit like a loose-fitting glove. Many varieties are smaller than oranges and some are seedless.

Mandarins, (*Citrus reticulata*) often called m*andarin oranges*, are small, mild-tasting and sweet. They do have some seeds, which makes them slightly less desirable for snacking when compared with seedless Clementines. Mandarin oranges have one of the longest seasons from January to May.

Many older people will have had tinned mandarins as a dessert. They used to be a popular canned fruit packed in syrup, often served with evaporated milk or laid in a circular pattern on a sponge flan and covered with sweet aspic for a dessert.

SATSUMAS

Satsumas (*Citrus unshiu*) are a variety of small mandarin oranges. They are seedless, sweet and juicy, and their slightly lighter coloured skin is loosely attached to the fruit, ensuring they are easy to peel. The peel's looseness makes them tender, so bruising can be difficult to detect.

The seedless Satsuma copes relatively well with the cold and is in season from November through to January.

CLEMENTINES

Clementines (*Citrus reticulata*) are the smallest type of mandarin. They are super sweet, seedless and have red-orange skins that are smooth and shiny. They are easy to peel.

Clementines and satsumas are often marketed interchangeably, although the difference is easy to detect since clementines have tight skins and satsumas have loose peels.

NADORCOTTS

Nadorcotts (*Citrus reticulata*) are the result of a chance cross-pollination of an unknown variety with Murcott Clementine. Discovered in 1982, they have a great depth of flavour, are small, easy to peel, have no pips and were cultivated as an alternative to satsumas and clementines. They have a good balance of sweetness and acidity, and originate from Afourer, Morocco.

KISHUS

The Kishu (*Citrus kinokuni* ex 'Tanaka') is a very small variety of bright orange mandarin with a snug-fitting peel. The fruit is sweet and thin skinned, and many varieties are seedless, although some do have seeds. They are ideal as a snack for young children, being a little larger than a walnut.

TANGERINES

While tangerines (*Citrus tangerina*) may be viewed as synonymous with mandarins by many people, tangerines are in reality a variety of mandarin which originally appeared in Tangier.

Tangerines have bright orange skins and are smaller than oranges, with looser peels. They are good for eating and adding to salads, and can also be juiced for a slightly sweeter and brighter take on classic orange juice. With a season running from November through to May, tangerines are available for longer than many citrus fruits.

TANGORS

Many oranges float, but Tangors (*Citrus reticulata*) – half orange and half tangerine – are so sweet and loaded with sugar that they will sink in a bowl of water. They are also called *Temple Oranges* and have a thick rind which is easy to peel. Their bright orange pulp is sour-sweet and full flavoured.

LEMONS

The lemon, (*Citrus limon*), is a species of the small evergreen tree in the flowering plant family Rutaceae. Its origin is unknown, although lemons are thought to have first grown in Assam (a region in North East India), Northern Myanmar (Burma) or China. A genomic study indicates that lemons were originally produced as a hybrid of the bitter orange and the citron.

Lemons entered Europe near Southern Italy no later than the second century AD, during Ancient Rome times, but they were not widely cultivated at that time. They were later introduced to Persia and then to Iraq and Egypt around 700 AD.

Lemons vary greatly in size and colour, from bright yellow to mellow green/yellow – and in the thickness of their peel and pith. Some have smooth skins, while others are knobbly, rough peeled, and their level of acidity differs depending on the variety. Lemon trees grow faster than orange trees, and they are usually more productive and will stand more neglect.

While most lemons are tart, acidic and astringent, they are also surprisingly refreshing. Good quality lemons are usually thin skinned, since those with thick skins will have less flesh, making them less juicy.

Lemons come in numerous varieties and are either sour or sweet. The two main types of sour lemons are the Eureka and the Lisbon. One of the most popular sweet lemons is the Meyer.

EUREKA

The Eureka (*Citrus limon* 'Eureka') lemon generally has a textured skin, and a short neck at one end. Probably originating from Italy, (perhaps from the Lunario variety) the Eureka lemon produces medium to large, oblong fruit with a small nipple at the stylar (flower) end and a thicker, rougher, tightly clinging rind. It is less thorny than Lisbon and Meyer lemons, and can be seedless or have very few seeds. Eureka is fast growing, with greenish-yellow pulp and considerably tolerant of colder weather, with short spells of temperatures down to -5°C (23°F). The tree has upright growing branches, dark green glossy foliage with strongly scented white flowers, and reaches a height of 4.5–7.5 metres (15–25 feet).

LISBON

The Lisbon (*Citrus limon*) lemon is one of the most widely cultivated lemons. Believed to be from a Gallego seedling selection of Portuguese origin, Lisbon lemon trees are vigorously growing with large, sometimes thorny, but upright, spreading branches. They are cultivated as both dwarf and standard trees, reaching a height of 7.5 metres (25 feet), with fruit hidden under dense, evergreen foliage.

Lisbon lemons have medium-sized, oblong fruits with a rounded stem end, no neck and a prominent nipple. The thin, smooth to medium-thick, tightly clinging rind is smooth and bright yellow when mature. It is finely pitted with oil glands that when scratched or rubbed, offer a strong citrusy aroma. The pale-yellow flesh is high in Vitamin C, has few to no seeds and is very juicy and acidic. Lisbon grows well in California and much of Southern Europe, but it is low yielding and short lived in India.

MEYER

The Meyer (*Citrus meyeri* 'Improved') was taken from China to the USA by Frank Meyer in 1908. By the mid- 1940s the Meyer was widely grown in California, when it was discovered that the majority of trees that were being cloned were symptomless carriers of the Citrus tristeza virus, which has killed millions of citrus trees across the globe. Most of the Meyer lemon trees in the United States were then destroyed to save the other citrus trees.

Work was conducted to find a virus-free version, and in 1975 the University of California released a certified virus-free version known as the 'Improved Meyer Lemon' which has now replaced the original strain.

This lemon produces a small, round or oval, yellow fruit up to 8 cm (3 inches) in diameter, with a smooth, thin skin and a less pronounced, short nipple. A hybrid of lemon and mandarin orange, the brilliant yellow peel has hints of light orange blush and the pulp is pale orange-yellow. Naturally sweet, they are highly fragrant, juicy, with rinds full of volatile oils that are used in cooking. Meyers grow in bunches of 6–10 lemons, hanging heavily down, and are the best lemon for taste and flavour.

Their pulp is low to moderate in acid, and each fruit may contain 8–12 small seeds. Meyer trees are small, often 1.8–3 metres (6–10 feet) high, with dark green shiny leaves and few thorns. They produce fragrant white flowers with a purple base. The cold resistant trees are prolific and grow a bush-like canopy.

The sweet flavoured Meyer lemon is becoming ever more popular in both consumer markets and restaurants.

Eureka, Lisbon and Meyer are just three of the most popular varieties of lemon – and here is a small selection of some of the others.

AMALFI

The special Italian Amalfi lemon (*Sfusato Amalfitano)* is a long, tapered variety about double the size of many other lemons. It has a thick wrinkled skin with an intense perfume and sweet, juicy flesh. Traditionally cultivated in terraced gardens, the special taste comes from the exposure to sea breezes and strong sun while being protected from cold, northern winds.

AVON

Avon (*Citrus limon*) was first noticed as a budded tree in 1934 in Florida. It produces heavy crops of fruit suitable for frozen concentrated juice and became a source of budwood for commercial propagation.

BEARSS

The Bearss lemon (*Citrus latifolia*) closely resembles the Lisbon. The trees are vigorous and tend to produce too many sprouts. It is also highly susceptible to diseases such as scab, greasy spot and oil spotting. Nonetheless it was propagated commercially by Libby, McNeill & Libby because its peel is rich in oil, and it constitutes a substantial proportion of Brazil's lemon crop.

BERNA

The Berna or Verna lemon (sometimes spelt 'Bernia' or 'Vernia') (*Citrus limon* 'Verna') is the second most widely grown cultivar in Spain, after the Fino. This Spanish variety of unknown origin may have been developed in Murcia from the Italian Monachello. The oval fruit is medium-sized, with a pronounced nipple, short neck and tightly clinging, somewhat rough skin.

Usually seedless, or with only a few seeds, and great juice, the fruit keeps well on the tree during winter, becoming fairly large. As well as in Spain, it is also grown in Algeria and Morocco, however in Florida it has been found to be deficient in acid, low in juice and susceptible to scab.

FEMMINELLO

Femminello Santa Teresa lemons, (*Citrus limon*) Siracusa or Sorrento lemons, are large, round or elongated, with a tapered nipple. This variety is the most common lemon in Italy. Its medium thick rind is bright yellow and dotted with deep oil glands that release a distinct, intense citrus aroma, leading to this lemon being the favourite for making limoncello. The pale yellow flesh is very juicy and contains few seeds.

These leading Italian cultivars produce medium-sized lemons that are rich in flavour, highly acidic, and with a slight sweetness. The trees are vigorous and almost thornless, fruiting all year but mainly late winter and spring. The fruit travels and stores well. Regulations applied to the Siracusa lemon forbid the use of waxes and/or fungicides post harvest, so the whole of the fruit is edible.

FINA OR PRIMOFIORI

The Fino or Primofiori (*Citrus limon* L. Burm. Fil) is listed as a synonym for Mesero Lemon and is the most popular lemon crop grown in Spain. It was developed in Murcia from ordinary lemon seeds of the Vega Alta del Segura. Moderately seeded, the Fino bears a spherical or oval fruit with a small nipple. It has a thin, smooth rind, pale in colour and has a high juice and acid content. The excessively thorny trees grow vigorously, attaining a large size. A spontaneous mutation of the Fino, the new lemon strain, Summer Prim, was detected in Murcia in 2005 and is now a protected variety with an expanding marketplace.

GENOA

The Genoa (*Citrus limon* L. Burm.f.) is almost identical to Eureka. An ovoid or oblong fruit with a blunt nipple, this medium-sized lemon has a yellow, medium-thick, tightly clinging peel. It has numerous seeds and grows on a thorny, cold-hardy tree. It is cultivated commercially in India, Chile and Argentina.

INTERDONATO

Interdonato lemons (*Citrus limon* L. Burm.f.) are a result of a cross between a citron and a local Italian lemon from Sicily. The name comes from Giovanni Interdonato, one of Garibaldi's colonels, who supposedly created it, but it might simply have been a spontaneous mutation in his garden. The resulting lemon is medium to large with a delicate, only mildly acidic flavour. The glossy skin is fine grained and tightly clinging, and the lemon has a characteristic large point at the end. The pulp is greenish-yellow, while the tree is vigorous and usually thornless.

MONACHELLO

Monachello (*Citrus limon* L. Burm.f.) is suspected of being a lemon citron hybrid. This medium sized elliptical fruit has a small nipple, and its tight yellow peel is thin and smooth except for large, sunken oil glands. The pulp is neither very juicy nor sharply acid. The tree is slow growing, almost thornless, not that vigorous, and has been extensively planted in Italy.

NEPALI

The Nepali Oblong (Assam, Pat Nebu) (*Citrus limetta Risso*) originated in Assam and resembles a citron. A long, elliptic fruit with greenish-yellow peel, a short nipple and smooth, glossy skin, this is very juicy with few or no seeds, and it fruits throughout the year. The tree is reasonably thorny and prolific and is grown commercially in India. A similar lemon, but without the distinct nipple, is the Nepali Round, a nearly-thornless tree that is reasonably prolific and cultivated in South India.

PERRINE

Perrine Lemonime (*Citrus limon* 'Lemonime') is a hybrid of West Indian lime and Genoa lemon. Named after Dr Henry Perrine for his contribution to the citrus industry in Florida, these small fruits are similar to limes, being 4–5 cm (1.5–2 inches) in diameter. Their thin yellow rind may have traces of pale green, and each fruit will have 3–10 seeds. With high acidity, close to that of a traditional lemon, juicy Perrine offers a lime-like, tart flavour. They are naturally resistant to lemon scab, but a hard frost will destroy them, so they have not experienced commercial success, being overtaken by Persian limes.

PONDEROSA

The Ponderosa (*Citrus maxima medica*) has a pear-shaped fruit with thick peel and leaves, indicating its origin as a lemon-citron hybrid. Not a true lemon, it has large, showy fruit, often the size of a grapefruit. Its low-growing habit and good tolerance to pruning and cutting all make it a popular ornamental tree. Grown as a domestic curiosity in preference to commercial planting, it is widely cultivated as an indoor potted plant in temperate regions. As it's very acidic, it can be used in cooking.

ROUGH LEMON

Rough Lemon (*Citrus jambhiri* 'Lush') is perhaps a lemon citron hybrid. Believed to have originated in North India, Portuguese explorers carried it at the end of the 15th Century first to Southeast Africa, then Europe, where the Spaniards took it to the New World. A cold-hardy citrus, the tree has been of great importance as a rootstock for the sweet orange, mandarin orange and grapefruit. It is no longer used as a rootstock for lemon in Florida because it is susceptible to blight and foot rot.

VILLAFRANCA AND OTHER LEMONS

Said to be of Sicilian origin, the Villafranca lemon (*Citrus limon* L. Burm.f.) is similar to the Lisbon lemon but ripens earlier. It was introduced to Florida around 1875 and later to California, and for many years was the leading cultivar in Florida, although it has recently been superseded by the Bearss. Villafranca is grown commercially in Israel and Argentina, but in India it is low yielding and short-lived.

Italian Amalfi (*Sfusato Amalfitano*) and Sicilian lemons (typically Femminello) are known for their good flavour, and while their peel may be thick or thin, they have strong zest which harbours their essential oils.

The Amalfi coast, south of Naples, has long been famous for its lemons, including the sfusato amalfitano, a large fruit, with juicy flesh, few seeds and a thick skin, full of highly perfumed essential oils. This variety has been recognised by being given a Protected Geographical Status.

Landowners in the Conca d'Oro, Sicily, poured resources into improving the soil and planting citrus groves and vineyards, making the Conca d'Oro more beautiful than before. Olives and vineyards were established in the drier parts of the landscape and citrus introduced to areas with a reliable water supply.

CHINOTTO

A long-established Italian pre-dinner drink is the apéritif Campari with orange juice. Campari was invented in 1860 by Gaspare Campari and gains its distinctive bitter taste from the highly acidic Chinotto, a citrus fruit unique to Liguria, the coastal strip running between Monaco and Pisa. Chinotto (*Citrus myrtilolia*) is referred to as the 'little dwarf from China', having been brought to Italy via the northern port of Savona by a sailor returning from the Far East in around 1500.

Chinotto was cross-pollinated and mutated, evolving into the unique variety identified as *Citrus aurantium var. amara subvar. Sinensis*. Today the fruit is commonly known as 'Chinotto di Savona'. Although its name refers to an origin in China, it is now thought to have originally come from Vietnam.

The slow growing Chinotto tree is unattractive when young, having a stunted appearance, but as it matures, it takes on an elegant, graceful shape. Its branches hang with bunches of tiny fruit, ready for harvest in August. Individual Chinotto rarely weigh more than 60 grams (2 oz) and the pungent skin and flesh imparts a distinctive 'love it or hate it' flavour to pastries, drinks, and marmalade.

Citrus grown in these cooler northern climes are especially bitter, which made them particularly popular for North European cuisine. Living on the edge of their temperature range, and susceptible to sudden frosts, the coast may allow the cultivation of sheltered pockets of citrus but move a couple of hundred metres up the hillside and the conditions become untenable. There are few citrus farms left in Liguria today.

Growers have their own special defences against pest invasions. Bottles filled with ammonia and a floating anchovy hung from branches are one such defence. This mixture is a tempting bait for wasps, flies and hornets, but since no sugar is added to the mix, pollinating bees take no notice of these insect traps.

Sailors in Italy knew that citrus prevented scurvy long before James Lind confirmed this in 1747, and barrels of Chinotto were kept onboard Italian ships, stored in casks of sea water to preserve these bitter lemons. Each Chinotto was cut in half, so the brine was in contact with the rind and flesh, to preserve both equally.

Candied Chinotto is manufactured in Savona and used in Christmas panettone. The fruit is soaked in brine for anything between four and 12 months, and then tipped into a turning drum with a slightly rough surface to remove a thin layer of rind to expose the Chinotto's pungent essential oils. The tough little Chinotto is then boiled for a minimum of three hours before being tipped into a solution of hot water with a 20 per cent sugar concentration.

This starts the candying process by removing the moisture from the fruit and replacing it with crystallised sugar. The fruit is kept at 60°C (140°F) to prevent it fermenting. Over some 10 days the water evaporates and the sugar is topped up. The crystallised fruit is then ready to eat. Although the skin remains slightly hard, the flesh melts in the mouth, with an intense, characteristic bittersweet taste, and leaves a slight fizzing sensation in the mouth.

Crystallised fruit was regarded as a comfit (confection) or sweetmeat, and was eaten with a sucket fork, a small metal utensil with a two or three-pronged fork at one end of the handle and a spoon bowl, usually of teaspoon size, at the other. A sucket fork is mentioned in Edward VI's inventory of 1549, but most of the few surviving English and American examples, which are usually made of silver, date from the late 17th Century.

The popularity of crystallised fruit diminished during and after the Second World War; this little gem could have been lost. But in the 1990s Savona reinvented itself as an Italian tourist port for cruise ships which inspired the council to look for a local symbol for the city, and the Chinotto was proposed.

Then they discovered that only 118 trees were growing in Liguria, so hundreds of new trees were planted. By 2004, Chinotto became a protected traditional product, and today it is found in a selection of delicious marmalades, liqueurs, amaretti biscuits and Christmas panettone.

Although today few people outside Liguria are familiar with Chinotto fruit, something of a cult-beverage status has developed for San Pellegrino's orange juice, which was launched in 1932, and bears the name *Chinotto*.

This carbonated drink is available in three flavours – as Classic Orange juice, Orange Amara (bitter), and Sweet Orange juice – to satisfy the preferences of different drinkers. All three have the distinctive presence of the unmistakable orange pulp, although the oranges used to flavour this drink come from Sicily.

San Pellegrino launched a new brand of the soft drink called *Chino* in 1986. And for those wanting something stronger, there is the sweet, sour and bitter Quaglia Liquore di Chinotto made with Chinotto.

LIMES

There are many species of citrus trees whose fruits are called *limes*, but the botanical complexity of the citrus genus itself, to which the majority of limes belong, makes it difficult to identify different species of lime across the world.

Members of this genus hybridise readily, and it is only recently that genetic studies have started to throw light on their botanical structure. Some so-called *limes* are not in fact limes in the true sense. The name *lime* comes from French *lime*, Arabic *līma*, and Persian *līmū* or 'lemon'.

The major cultivated species of limes, Key lime (*Citrus aurantifolia*), Kaffir lime (*Citrus hystrix*) and Persian or Tahitian lime (*Citrus latifolia*), are all hybrids. Other limes are a result of cross-fertilisation of species such as citron (*Citrus medica*), mandarin orange (*Citrus reticulata*), pomelo (*Citrus maxima*) and/or micrantha (*Citrus micrantha*).

Most limes are typically round, 3–6 cm (1.2–2.4 inches) in diameter and contain acidic juice vesicles. The skin of the lime is thin and green or yellow/green colour. The pulp is pale green and filled with a very sharp acid juice. Limes are a rich source of Vitamin C, sour and are often used to accent the flavours of foods and beverages. They are grown all year round.

Raw limes are an average of 88 per cent water, 10 per cent carbohydrates and less than 1 per cent each of fat and protein. Nutritionally, only their Vitamin C content at 35 per cent of the daily value per 100 gm (3.5 oz) serving is significant. Lime juice contains slightly less citric acid than lemon juice (about 47 gm/l), nearly twice the citric acid of grapefruit juice, and about five times the amount of citric acid found in orange juice.

Limes are the most acidic of all citrus fruit. And they have a higher sugar content than lemons. The best limes are deep green in colour and should be stored in a cool location, away from sunlight, or their flavour will diminish as they change to a lemon colour. Lime juice may be squeezed from fresh limes, or purchased in bottles, either unsweetened or sweetened.

Contact with lime peel or lime juice followed by exposure to ultraviolet light may lead to *phytophotodermatitis*, which is sometimes called 'margarita photodermatitis' or 'lime disease' (not to be confused with Lyme disease). Bartenders handling limes and other citrus fruits while preparing cocktails may develop *phytophotodermatitis*, the symptoms of which can include inflammation of the skin, oedema or blisters.

Lime peel contains higher concentrations of furanocoumarins than lime pulp (by one or two orders of magnitude), and so lime peels are considerably more phototoxic than lime pulp. Persian limes appear to be more phototoxic than Key limes.

LYME DISEASE
Lyme disease is caused by bacteria, *Borrelia burgdorferi* that are transmitted to humans through a bite from an infected tick. Ticks can also bite dogs but there is a Lyme vaccine for dogs. Lyme disease has nothing to do with lime disease.

KEY LIME

Key lime (*Citrus aurantifolia*) are also known as West Indies lime or Mexican lime. The Indo-Malayan region has cultivated these fruit for thousands of years, both as a fruit and for its decorative foliage.

Historically, Arab traders brought Key lime from the Far East through Palestine to Southern Europe and the Mediterranean. It is believed that Columbus took lime to the Americas, where it flourished in southern Florida. Today many Key limes come from Mexico.

Thin-skinned Key limes are smaller and have more seeds than the common Persian lime. Their distinctive flavour and acidity make them sought after for famous dishes such as Key Lime Pie, although as they ripen and turn yellow, their acid content reduces, resulting in a sweeter fruit.

KAFFIR LIME

One of the most aromatic of herbs, Kaffir lime leaf (*Citrus hystrix*) is a key ingredient in Southeast Asian and Thai cooking, where it is added to curries, stir fries and stews. The Kaffir lime fruit is bitter and not consumed, but it is also found in many Asian cleaning products.

PERSIAN LIME

Persian lime (*Citrus latifolia*) is also known as the Bearss lime or Tahiti lime. It is a hybrid triploid cross between key lime and lemon. Persian lime is the most widely commercially cultivated lime species. Often sold while green, it turns yellow as it ripens. The tree is nearly thornless. The fruit is around 6 cm (2.4 inches) in diameter, often with a slightly nippled end and no seeds.

GRAPEFRUIT

Grapefruit flesh comes in various shades of yellow, red, pink, and cream (called white) but these colours do not refer to the skin of the fruit. Taste and texture do not materially differ whichever variety is chosen. Most grapefruit have yellow skins, but some, especially those with pink or red flesh, will have rosy speckles or reddish patches on the peel. Grapefruit are usually seedless, but some will have the occasional seed.

There is some mystery or perhaps controversy, over the origins of grapefruit, partly because of their name. Pummelo (*Citrus maxima*) is one of the three original citrus strains. In different countries Pummelo can also be called *pomelo*, *pamplemousse* or *shaddock*.

Some sources cite the shaddock as a citrus that is believed to have grown in Asia as early as 100 BC (BCE). A chance hybrid of two Asian plants, the shaddock and sweet orange, is said to have resulted in the grapefruit.

So-called because they grow in bunches like oversized grapes, grapefruit trees are a spectacular sight with the large yellow fruit hanging among the dark green leaves.

There are several versions of how grapefruit reached the western world and the dates are somewhat random.

One tale recounts that the fruit was originally named by British naturalist Sir Hans Sloane. During his mission as a physician in Jamaica, he noted about 800 new species of plants. In 1696 his catalogue of plants was published in Latin and there he attributed the fruit's name to Captain Shaddock, a captain of an East India ship.

According to Sloane, Shaddock brought pomelo seeds to Jamaica and Barbados, as he described in 1707, in his voyage to the islands of Madeira, Barbados, Neves, St Christopher's and Jamaica with the natural history of the herbs and trees. The shaddocks in Barbados flourished and surpassed those of Jamaica in goodness.

Another report says that Captain Shaddock purportedly brought the first grapefruit to Barbados in 1649.

In 1750, Welsh naturalist Griffith Hughes discovered what he called the *forbidden fruit* in Welchman Hall Gully, a lush tropical forest located in a collapsed cave on Barbados. Today this Bajan gully, with its spectacular vegetation and several troops of wild monkeys, is a natural park open to the public and well worth a visit.

According to local legend, Barbados lays claim to the original grapefruit in the Caribbean. The story goes that farmers in Barbados accidentally cross bred sweet orange with pomelo in the 1800s. Upon tasting the fruit, one Jamaican farmer thought the flavour was similar to a grape, so he called it grapefruit and the name stuck.

The names *shaddock* and *grapefruit* are often used incorrectly. Grapefruit, or *pomelo* in Spanish, is the species *Citrus paradisi*, while shaddock, sometimes called *pummelo*, is *Citrus maxima,* and is often referred to as *Chinese* or *Asian grapefruit*. Shaddocks look more like giant pears and have a firm or crunchy pulp and thick peel. And then to add to the confusion, shaddock is the name given in Australia to the large pomelo.

Grapefruit did not gain its individual status until the 1830s, and only started to become popular towards the end of the 19th Century, having formerly only been grown as an ornamental plant. The grapefruit eventually migrated from the New World to Spain but didn't become a staple of the Spanish diet until recently. China is now the world's leading producer of grapefruit, followed by Spain and the USA.

With the increasing popularity of this fruit and thus demand, there has been much cross-pollination, and there are now many different types of grapefruit, categorised by colour. Here are just over a dozen of the most popular.

WHITE GRAPEFRUIT

The White grapefruit (*Citrus paradisi*) is yellow skinned with cream coloured flesh. This is the least sweet variety and is a favourite for its sweet/tart balance coupled with an intense, vibrant aroma and clear, colourless juice.

PINK GRAPEFRUIT

The Pink grapefruit (*Citrus paradisi*) variety has a pinkish flesh and sometimes pink flecks on its yellow skin. Regarded as one of the most delicious, best tasting grapefruits ever, between sweet and sour, it is mildly tangy and great for juicing.

RED GRAPEFRUIT

Red grapefruit (*Citrus paradisi*) has the least complex taste and can be very bitter. The red colour comes from lycopene, a cancer-fighting antioxidant that helps to prevent free radical damage and premature ageing of cells. It also contains the antioxidant known as beta-carotene.

ORO BLANCO

Oro Blanco, or *white gold* (*Citrus paradisi* Macfadyen) is a cross between a pomelo and standard white grapefruit. It has a thick, yellow skin and is almost completely seedless. Juicy and sweet, with virtually no bitterness or acidity in the flesh, it tastes delicious.

DUNCAN GRAPEFRUIT

One of the oldest varieties of grapefruit, Duncan (*Citrus paradisi* Macfadyen) is a large, yellow skinned Florida fruit. It is very juicy and has an incredible flavour. However, because it is full of seeds, it is generally used for juicing. A high-quality fruit, it ripens early and is sweeter than seedless varieties.

FLAME GRAPEFRUIT

When sliced open, Flame grapefruit (*Citrus paradisi* Macfadyen) reveals a dark pink flesh that while more pronounced than some other red grapefruit, is not really a bright red. It is juicy and very sweet, with few or no seeds. The fruit ripens on the trees from November to May and can remain on the tree for months without deterioration.

TEXAS RED GRAPEFRUIT

The Texas red grapefruit (*Citrus paradisi*) was named the official state fruit in 1993. It is grown in the part of southern Texas called the Lower Rio Grande Valley.

RUBY SWEET

The Ruby Sweet (*Citrus paradisi*) is a portmanteau category for the Ruby Red, Ray Ruby and Star Ruby, three popular varieties of grapefruit commonly called Ruby Sweet that are easy to grow in Florida.

RUBY RED

Grapefruit were first shipped commercially in Texas in 1920, but then in 1929 a red grapefruit was discovered growing on a pink variety. Named Ruby Red, (*Citrus paradisi*) and patented, this new mutant was associated with real commercial success, making the Texas Red Grapefruit Industry soar. Using radiation to trigger mutations, new varieties were developed to retain the red tones which typically faded to pink.

There were several varieties of red grapefruit being shipped from Texas, and it soon became hard to keep track of them – so all Texas red grapefruit were marketed under the name of Ruby Red.

RAY RUBY

Ray Ruby (*Citrus paradisi* Macfadyen) is a mutation of Ruby Red discovered in a Texas grove in 1970. This improved hybrid has redder flesh, fewer seeds and more of a blush to its peel. The fruit is a good size and shape with excellent yields and was released for sale in 1986.

STAR RUBY

Both tart and sweet, the Star Ruby (*Citrus paradisi* Macfadyen) sports a smooth yellow skin with a pink blush. Its flesh is the darkest of the red varieties. The fruit is smaller than some grapefruit and, with its low acid content and sweeter taste, it is a popular variety.

Star Ruby is more widely known than Rio Red, but can be somewhat delicate with limited resistance to sun exposure. As it is less vigorous, Star Ruby can be more difficult to grow than other varieties.

RIO RED

Rio Red (*Citrus paradisi* Macfadyen) is a large fruit with a slightly pebbled surface with a pink blush. This juicy fruit has deep red flesh and not only gets its colour from lycopene, an antioxidant that is good for the cardiovascular system, but also contains Vitamin C and potassium which are good for the heart.

The Rio Red variety was, in 2007, the Texas grapefruit with the registered trademarks Rio Star and Ruby Sweet. Sometimes promoted as 'Reddest' and 'Texas Choice', the Rio Red is a mutation bred for better fruit and juice qualities, and is a deeper red colour. Rio Red will typically produce fruit for 30–40 years or more and matures mid-to-late season.

RIO STAR

The Rio Star (*Citrus paradisi*) combines the Rio Red and the Star Ruby grapefruit. It contains an overall blush on the outside skin with a deep red flesh colour inside, far more red than Ruby Red and a very sweet flesh.

WHITE MARSH SEEDLESS

The White Marsh Seedless (*Citrus paradisi*) has yellow skin and pale flesh with a sweet, acidic taste. First planted in Florida around 1860, it is one of the most popular grapefruit available on the global market. From the outside, it looks like a large lemon, as it is round and yellow. From the inside, the creamy yellow flesh has a well-balanced sweet sugar content and acidity, with a classic, juicy flavour. Marsh Seedless accounts for some 40 per cent of the commercial grapefruit production in Florida.

Marsh seedless grapefruit also comes in varieties that include Marsh Pink and Ruby Red Marsh. Pink Marsh has yellow skin and flesh that is light pink in colour. It is less sweet than White Marsh and with less acidic flesh. The Ruby Red Marsh has red flesh, a yellow to pale red skin and a taste that is sweeter and less acidic than the White Marsh.

THOMPSON GRAPEFRUIT

Thompson grapefruit has been around since 1913 and is another name for the Marsh Pink. This seedless variety is found on a tree that grows up to 7.5 metres (25 feet) and matures from October through to February, although it can remain on the tree for several months. It looks and tastes almost identical to the Marsh seedless and is grown widely in Texas and Florida.

LAVENDER GEM

Lavender Gem grapefruit is a combination of a grapefruit and tangelo. It has a lemon-yellow or pink blush skin and looks like a miniature grapefruit. With few seeds in its pinkish-blue flesh, it has a light, delicate flavour. Sometimes called the *pink tangelo* or just *tangelo*, it is extremely juicy, and good for marinades and fruit salads.

MELOGOLD GRAPEFRUIT

Melogold is a hybrid between a pomelo and grapefruit created by Californian farmers in the late 1950s. This variety has few seeds, comes in various sizes and can be quite large. It has become a popular choice for those wanting an extremely juicy fruit with a taste similar to an orange plus an added hint of grapefruit flavour. The smooth rind is easily peeled and this fruit can be eaten like an orange.

SWEETIES GRAPEFRUIT

Sweeties grapefruit, which are green in colour and have pale flesh, as their name implies, taste very sweet. They were produced by combining a pomelo with a standard grapefruit.

With so many varieties, it is hardly surprising to learn that grapefruit are one of the most popular citrus fruit, especially as they have numerous health benefits.

OTHER CITRUS

There are many other, rarer citrus fruits such as citron, ugli, yuzu, pomelo, Buddha's hand, kinnow, rangpur and more.

CITRON

A large fruit, the citron (*citrus medica)* has a thick peel which can be dried and added to pastries and cakes. This rind may be wrinkled or smooth, and will be green when unripe and turn yellow-orange when overripe. The pith can be preserved or cooked in sugar and eaten as a dessert. The slightly bitter flesh is usually limited to around 25 per cent of the fruit. Because of its particular acid flavour, it is perfect for making sweet juice as well as being paired with savoury dishes.

UGLI

The Jamaican tangelo, also known by the proprietary name *Ugli fruit*, is a citrus variety that arose on that island through the natural hybridization of a tangerine or orange with a grapefruit (or pomelo) and is thus called a *tangelo*. As a hybrid species, it is usually represented as *Citrus reticulata paradisi*, and today is mainly grown in Jamaica.

The tangelo is usually slightly larger than a grapefruit, but this varies. Blemishes on the light-green surface turn orange when the fruit is at peak ripeness. The rind is fragrant, and the very juicy flesh has few seeds.

The taste is often described as sourer than an orange but tends towards the sweet side of the tangerine rather than the bitter side of its grapefruit lineage. The fruit is seasonal and is usually available in Europe and the United States from November to April.

YUZU

Yuzu (*Citrus junos,* from Japanese) is called *yuja* (from Korean 유자) in Korean cuisine. The fruit looks similar to a small grapefruit with an uneven skin, and can be either yellow or green, turning to orange depending on the degree of ripeness. Yuzu fruit, which are very aromatic, typically range between 5.5 cm (2 inches) and 7.5 cm (3 inches) in diameter. However, they can be as large as a regular grapefruit (up to 10 cm (4 inches) or larger). Yuzu forms an upright shrub or small tree, usually with many prominent thorns. The large leaves are aromatic and look similar to the Kaffir lime.

POMELO

The Pomelo, or Shaddock in Australia, (*Citrus maxima* or *Citrus grandis*), is the largest citrus fruit from the Rutaceae family. As one of the original citrus species, it is a natural, rather than a hybrid citrus fruit, and one from which the rest of cultivated citrus have been hybridized. Native to Asia, it is similar in appearance to a large grapefruit, and is ultimately the source fruit of all grapefruit hybrids. (*Pomelo* is the Spanish for 'grapefruit'.)

The typical pomelo is much larger than the grapefruit, being up to 15–25 cm (6–10 inches) in diameter. It will have a yellow or pale lime-green skin when ripe. There are two varieties of pomelo: a sweet one with white flesh, and a sour kind with pinkish flesh, the latter more likely to be used as an altar decoration, rather than eaten.

The thick, bitter pith (albedo) is easy to peel. The taste is like a sweet, mild grapefruit, with none of the grapefruit's bitterness. With mellow flesh, it is a popular fruit to add to salads. Pomelo peel can be used to make marmalade, candied, or dipped in chocolate. In Brazil the thick skin is made into a sweet conserve.

In large parts of Southeast Asia, where Citrus maxima is native, it is a popular dessert, often eaten raw and sprinkled with, or dipped in, a salt mixture, or in Sri Lanka, sprinkled with sugar. This popular fruit is used in many festive celebrations throughout Southeast Asia, such as the mid-autumn or mooncake festivals.

Sometimes called the *Chinese Grapefruit*, pomelo is an important part of Chinese New Year celebrations.

BUDDHA'S HAND

Buddha's Hand (*Citrus medica* var. sarcodactylis), or the 'Fingered citron', is an unusually shaped citron variety whose fruit is segmented into finger-like sections, resembling those seen on representations of Buddha. The different cultivars of this citron variety form a gradient from 'open-hand' types with outward-splayed segments to 'closed-hand' types, in which the 'fingers' are kept together. It is believed to originate from the Far East, probably China or India.

The fruit is highly fragrant and is used predominantly in the Far East for perfuming rooms and personal clothing. It is also given as a religious offering in Buddhist temples. In China, Buddha's Hand fruit is a symbol of happiness, longevity and good fortune, and a traditional New Year's gift.

Unlike other citrus fruits, most varieties of Buddha's Hand fruit contain no pulp or juice, although they have an exquisite form and aroma. The zest can be eaten as a flavouring for desserts and savoury dishes or candied as a sweet.

KINNOW

The Kinnow is a mandarin hybrid of two citrus cultivars – King (*Citrus nobilis*) and Willow Leaf (*Citrus deliciosa*) - grown extensively in the Punjab regions of India and Pakistan where plants can reach a height of 10.5 metres (35 feet). Kinnow trees are highly productive, so it is not uncommon to find 1,000 fruit per tree. The fruit peels easily and has a high juice content.

RANGPUR

The Rangpur, (*Citrus limonia* or *Citrus reticulata medica*), sometimes called the *Rangpur lime*, *Mandarin lime* or *Lemandarin*, is a hybrid between the mandarin orange and the citron. It has a very acidic taste and an orange coloured peel and flesh. The Rangpur is found in Bangladesh, India and South China.

Chapter 4.

HOW CITRUS ARE GROWN AND HARVESTED

Although citrus are grown across vast areas of the globe, because there are so many different types found in a variety of climates, their cultivation and harvesting are varied and often specific to the individual type of fruit.

In addition, the citrus fruit market is rapidly changing. In the 1970s Italy was a principal European producer, but now in the 21st Century, Spain is the leading producer in Europe, and accounts for a quarter of the global citrus fruit production.

Apart from the traditional citrus suppliers in China, Florida, California and Brazil, other countries now making their mark in the citrus field, as well as Spain. They include Australia, Egypt, Turkey and Uruguay, and some longer-standing sources such as Portugal, Morocco and South Africa.

CITRUS GROWTH

The flowering of citrus in subtropical regions usually lasts for about a month, while in tropical zones the trees can produce flowers all year round. Although thousands of flowers will open, very few, perhaps five per cent, will set fruit. And then excessively high temperatures or prolonged dry spells can lead to fruitlets dropping. The fruit will take from 6–18 months to grow to maturity depending on the climate and particular species. Hamlin and Navel oranges can be ready for picking six to eight months after flowering, while Valencia oranges are not harvested until at least 12 months after flowering.

Citrus fruits ripen on the tree, not after harvest like many other fruit. Oranges and lemons can be left on the tree for several extra months after they are mature. In ‘tree storage’ they will remain in good condition until picked. Mandarins or tangerines can be left on the tree for one to two months after reaching maturity; oranges can be left for five to six months; and grapefruit will store on the tree for up to eight months once mature.

Late orange crops and grapefruit will often have two crops on the tree at the same time, with both fruitlets and the blooms of the new crop alongside the mature fruits.

DISEASES, INSECT PESTS AND MITES

As with all trees, citrus are susceptible to a variety of diseases and viruses, some of which can be spread by humans budding trees with diseased buds.

Small fruitlets can be vulnerable to superficial peel damage by wind and insects. Post-bloom rains can lead to skin blemishes and insect attack. Wind scars also allow entry of waterborne fungal spores.

Individual citrus trees may carry pathogens or diseases that are detrimental to tree growth and fruit production and may affect neighbouring groves. Considerable losses can be caused by bud-transmitted diseases.

As major producers of citrus, the United States has taken key steps to control such diseases. The Californian citrus growers were among the first to recognise the damage caused, and in 1937 they formed a co-operative program to control these diseases. Texas followed suit in 1948, and in 1953 Florida's State Budwood Certification Program was introduced to minimise such problems. Only by using cuttings or budwood from pathogen-tested trees that are protected in greenhouses and are under inspection can the citrus industry achieve any degree of protection from harmful pathogens.

What is perhaps the most destructive disease, citrus tristeza virus (commonly known as 'CTV') is spread by aphids and particularly infects trees grown on sour orange rootstock, that is the root part of a grafted tree. This rootstock is rarely used these days precisely because of its susceptibility to this menace.

CTV originated in China and has travelled around the globe through the sale of infected budwood. The disease leads to the rapid decline or death of trees grafted into sour oranges rootstock.

Unfortunately, it can affect whole groves, leading to all the trees having to be grubbed up and the groves re-planted with trees grafted on alternative rootstocks. *Poncirus trifoliate* is a bitter Japanese orange that is frost hardy, and so far has proved resistant to CTV, so is becoming increasingly used as a reliable rootstock.

The Citrus Tristeza Agency was formed in California in 1963 with the aim of eradicating CTV. While CTV is still around, the activities of the Citrus Tristeza Agency have resulted in a very low level of CTV in California.

Another disease that commonly attacks is the citrus psyllid, a sap-sucking insect which originated in southern Asia and causes a serious citrus disease called *greening*. This disease, which produces sour, misshapen green fruit, was found in Brazil in 1942. By 1998 it was detected in Florida, and today it has spread to many other States. Recently in California, a tiny stingless parasitic wasp that is a natural enemy of psyllid has been used to combat this disease.

More than one thousand different insect pests and mites attack citrus trees across the globe, often causing considerable financial loss to growers. Aphids, black and white flies damage new growth and suck the sap from leaves.

There is also a range of fruit sucking moths with specialised probosces which they use to pierce the fruit in order to feed at night. Grasshoppers can be found chewing the peel of small fruit.

There are over 4,000 species of fruit flies across the globe. These are found in the Orient, the Mediterranean, South America and Mexico. They lay their eggs under the fruit rind, which when they hatch, attack the mature fruit, having a seriously deleterious effect on the economies of citrus cultivation.

Citrus thrips, minute winged insects which not only eat crops, but also carry viruses, are a serious pest for citrus fruits, especially in Californian and Indian orchards. And mites cause damage to lemons, grapefruit and Florida oranges.

As they seek to produce quality crops across the globe, citrus growers have an ongoing battle with these numerous diverse enemies from the plant and animal worlds.

Not so much a disease, as an irrational fear, a number of societies have believed that the worst thing that could happen was if a woman touched an orange tree. They thought the foliage might wilt, the fruit drop and the tree die.

In the early 18th Century, when nearly all German princes were growing oranges in their palaces, Johannes Volckamer of Nuremberg, in his *Neurenbergische Hesperiden*, described how women could cause whole trees to die.

"Many will deride this as something foolish," said Volckamer, "and I myself should not have believed in it had it not caused the undoing of some of my most valuable trees. Once, in winter, I noticed a woman of my gardener's household seated upon a beautiful orange tree in full bloom. The next day, the tree started drying up from the top downwards, and so rapid was the progress of the disease that in the course of a few days it had infected every single branch, causing all the leaves to wilt and die."

Some say that Volckamer did not appreciate the effect of a heavy frost on citrus.

CLIMATIC FACTORS

Hailstorms, untimely incessant rains or frosts can also have an adverse effect on citrus production. Losses due to freezes can to some extent be mitigated by using gas heaters and irrigation in orchards.

Lightning kills as many orange trees as any disease. Central inland Florida has more thunderstorms than any other area in the United States, and the trees on Florida's Ridge are an obvious target for the bolts to strike.

Wind is also a problem as it can damage branches, by whipping them against one another. If this happens when the tiny oranges are developing, minor blemishes can become major by the time the fruit has matured.

HARVESTING

Harvesting involves the removal of the fresh fruit from the tree once it has completed its growth and development. Given that citrus fruits ripen on the tree and not after harvest, they should not be removed from the tree until their growth and development have been completed.

All citrus fruit must be handled with great care while being harvested to ensure they are not damaged during the picking and packing processes and to prevent bruises and cuts to the skins as the fruit need to be wholesome, firm, intact and free from bruises, cuts or damage.

Oranges may be completely orange in colour or may have patches of green skin. Oranges produced in the tropics may be wholly green when ripe. Lemons can be a bright yellow, or a pale yellow with green. Limes are green, from true emerald to a pale olive or a vibrant chartreuse hue. Most grapefruit have yellow skins, but some, especially those with pink or red flesh, will have rosy speckles or reddish patches on the peel.

Citrus fruit are harvested throughout the year, depending on their variety and location. In tropical regions some fruit are picked while green, as they may not turn orange if the temperature does not fall at night.

Global harvesting of oranges takes place throughout the year, with key types such as Valencias being harvested from June to November and Navels from November to May in the Northern Hemisphere.

The heaviest lemon pickings are usually from March to April with lighter harvests in August and September. Lemons are picked when green skinned. They are measured and graded for size, the winter lemons usually being larger than the summer crop. Lemons may be cured in the packhouse to change the skin colour from green to a light yellow.

When ripe, lemons will normally have a minimum of 25 per cent juice content, and oranges between 30 and 45 per cent. Limes usually have a minimum juice content of 40+ per cent when mature.

Fruit size will depend on the specific variety of citrus, from the very small kumquat and kishu through to the large pomelo.

PICKING

The position where the fruit grows on the tree will have some influence on the way it is picked.

'Ground fruit'– that is, oranges that can be reached and picked from the ground – are not as sweet as fruit that has grown higher on the tree, as the higher fruit will usually get more sunshine. Outside fruit is sweeter than inside fruit, again possibly because it gets more sun. In the Northern Hemisphere, oranges on the south side of a tree are sweeter than those grown on the east or west, and oranges on the north side are the least sweet.

The same pattern is found in the quantity of juice and Vitamin C. And oranges are less tart the closer they are grown to the equator.

Since there may be blooms, fruitlets and mature fruit on the tree at the same time, manual harvesting is usually favoured. This allows the pickers to select the ripe fruit and leave those that are not yet mature for a future date, while not damaging blooms. Although this is arduous and time-consuming work, careful harvesting and handling minimises fruit injury and helps maintain high quality.

Many citrus are best removed by first twisting or bending the stem, and then pulling the fruit. This usually leaves a five-pointed or five-lobed calyx attached. The calyx will normally be green on freshly picked fruit, but can become grey-green to beige on fruit harvested some time ago.

Tangerines have to be removed from the tree with a pair of clippers, or a plug will pull out of the skin. This means that picking tangerines takes much longer than picking oranges, which can be done with a flick of the wrist.

As blood oranges are delicate, pickers use small secateurs to clip the oranges from the trees without damaging the fruit, working at a frantic pace as they weave in and out of the branches. The ground becomes scattered with fallen oranges, some of which will be attacked and devoured by insects, exposing the red flesh, like gruesome wounds.

Other tender citrus are clipped with the stem cut off close to the fruit with secateurs so that the skin is not damaged. Corsican clementines, which are sold with a leaf or two attached, are snipped with pruners because removal of the leaf endangers ripping the peel.

Pickers may use a ladder to reach higher fruit on tall trees, collecting their harvest in a canvas bag slung over the shoulder. When the bag is full, the fruit will be taken and tipped into crates for transport to the packing house. Careful handling helps to minimise fruit damage and so reduce rejection of part of the harvest.

In Florida, workers hand pick fruit, placing it in large bags which are then loaded on to specialised vehicles called *goats*. Harvested fruit from the groves then goes to roadside tractors and is transported to packhouses. There it is washed, graded and packed. There are about 40 packhouses and 20 citrus processing plants in Florida.

Oranges and mandarins will be shipped straight after picking so that they do not dry out, while lemons may be left undisturbed in a shaded grove for a day or two to allow slight water loss and so help avoid injury to the peel.

Damaged fruit cannot be sold in the whole fruit markets but is shipped to the juicing factories instead.

CURING

Any fruit picked early may need to be cured before being sold, the curing time varying depending on the citrus variety.

The water content of fruit peel determines the turgidity of the rind tissues, which in turn affects the extent of any injuries or damage after harvest. When fruit is harvested early in the day or in wet weather, it can then develop bruises or brown spots on the rind.

Curing is a pre-treatment that allows the slight removal of moisture from the peel before running the fruit on the packing line, so it becomes suitable for mechanical handling. This curing can be achieved by keeping the fruit in the shade at ambient conditions to allow it to dry. Lemons are usually cured by being held at 15–17°C (59–63°F) for one to two days.

DE-GREENING

Many fruits such as apples and pears, contain high levels of starch and 'breathe', or continue to ripen for some time after being picked. But citrus does not contain this starch, so it needs to ripen on the tree. It will not ripen further once it has been picked.

The flavedo, or outer skin, contains both orange and green pigments. Orange pigments or carotenoids produce yellow, orange and reddish-orange colours. The green colour comes from chlorophyll. The external colour of citrus fruit is not a reliable indication of internal maturity. Some oranges can be ripe while still green skinned.

Consumers prefer brightly coloured oranges and mandarins and are willing to pay a premium for such fruit. They see green-coloured oranges, although they may be mature, as being of poorer quality or unripe, and so they fetch lower prices.

The most attractive colours for citrus fruit are found in those grown in dry climates, where days are warm and nights are cool. A night-time temperature in the grove of between 5–13°C (41–55°F) will promote the desired orange colour by stimulating a decline in chlorophyll.

Bermuda has warm days, and ideal cool night-time temperatures to turn skins orange, so it produces some of the most beautiful oranges.

Citrus fruit are harvested throughout the year, depending on their variety, but in tropical regions where the temperature does not fall at night, oranges are picked while green, as they may never turn golden. Thailand, with its hot climate, has green mature oranges, and so does Jamaica.

Valencias are often seen as the best of American oranges, but at some time during the season may have mottled green skins, leading to a perceived lower value.

SURFACE COATINGS

Waxes or other coatings are used for polishing and improving the sheen of the fruit while reducing water loss. 'Wax' has become the generic term, whether the coating includes wax or not.

Common waxes are carnauba, paraffin and oxidised polyethylene. Carnauba is extracted from the leaves of the *Copernica prunifera* palm, which is native to Brazil. Oxidised polyethylene is an ethylene polymer. And paraffin is a hard-white crystalline wax from the petroleum industry.

Although these waxes are considered safe for consumption, many people prefer not to ingest this coating if they are using the peel. Supermarkets usually offer the alternative of unwaxed fruit, such as lemons or Seville oranges for marmalade making. If unwaxed fruit is not available, waxed fruit can be rinsed in hot water and scrubbed with a stiff vegetable brush.

PACKHOUSES

Packhouses are an important integral part of the citrus industry. Here fresh citrus is prepared ready for shipping to the market. An automated packhouse will manage mechanised handling, de-greening, pre-sizing, removing trash, grading, washing, rinsing, cool storage (to improve shelf life), labelling and packing ready for shipment. Small fruit, such as satsumas, may be weighed and then netted before shipping.

If skins do not turn orange naturally, de-greening can be used solely to improve the aesthetic value of the fruit, by allowing the carotenoids in the skins to show through. De-greening does not help to extend the fruit's keeping-quality, but has become a common commercial practice to improve its value in the fruit market.

Both orange and green pigments float in a clear enzyme called chlorophyllase, which will destroy chlorophyll on contact but has no effect on anything else. Chlorophyll is protected from this enzyme by a thin membrane called a *tonoplast*. In colder weather the tonoplast loses its strength and breaks down, and the enzyme gets at the chlorophyll and destroys it. The green peel becomes orange.

It would seem simple enough to put green oranges in a refrigerator until they turn orange. Unfortunately, the membrane that protects the chlorophyll from the enzyme no longer reacts in the same way once an orange has been picked.

So, green or partly green oranges are put in chambers with ethylene gas for several days. This gas enables the membrane that protects the chlorophyll to breakdown, thus allowing the fruit to turn orange.

In the past in America, an alternative method to the use of ethylene was to dye the orange skins, but not surprisingly consumers tended to avoid dyed oranges, especially when they were stamped in purple letters “Color Added”.

De-greening is done before washing the fruit in warm soapy water, brushing it with palmetto-fibre brushes and drying it with foam-rubber squeegees and jets of hot air. Brushed again with nylon bristles to bring out their natural shine, the fruit are then coated with a thin layer of edible wax, replacing the natural wax lost during the washing process, to prevent shrivelling within hours.

Oranges and other citrus are then graded. Split or rotting fruit are discarded. Those with blemished skins or with wind burns or other superficial damages are removed and sent to juicing plants.

As they move down the line, the oranges can bounce like rubber balls without damage, but fingernails can rupture the surface oil cells, so packers wear gloves. Oranges are packed at around 200 oranges per standard box.

Chapter 5.

WHERE DIFFERENT CITRUS ARE GROWN

Wherever there is a tropical or subtropical climate, there is potential for growing citrus, and given the popularity of these fruit, it is hardly surprising to find them cultivated around the globe. According to the Indian informational website World Blaze (2018), the leading producers of citrus in the world are as follows.

Brazil is the world's largest citrus fruit producer with a total of 21 million tons per annum for all citrus fruits together. Of this, 1.6 tons are limes, the majority of which are exported. Brazil has a large Citrus Belt which includes the state of Sao Paulo. It is said that 35 per cent of oranges grown globally come from Brazil, and many Brazilian oranges are juiced.

In the 1990s the large Brazilian processors acquired plants in Florida, and within a decade they controlled nearly half the processing capacity of that State. Through efficiency, extensive planting, technological know-how and integrated supply chains, Brazil now dominates the global orange juice market. In addition, Brazil produces more than half the world's lemon juice.

China is the second largest producer of all citrus fruit, with around 20 million tons per annum. There has been a 20 per cent growth in China's citrus production in the last 50 years, a large proportion being grapefruit, limes and lemons, although only a very small amount of their citrus is exported.

The USA is the world's largest producer of grapefruit. The States' total citrus production amounts to around 10 million tons, including substantial lime and lemon crops. California, Arizona, Texas, and Florida are major lemon growing regions. Most citrus in the USA are for home consumption and go to producing juices, the preferred way of using citrus.

Mexico is an important grower of citrus, with production from Nuevo Leon alone, one of Mexico's federal entities, meeting the demands for exports to foreign countries. Although it has some problems with inconsistencies in climate, which can have detrimental effects on crops, almost 2 million tons of limes and lemons are exported annually to the USA.

Southern coastal regions of Spain are well known for their sunny climate and highly fertile soil, so it is not surprising that country produces almost 6 million tons of citrus per annum, some 15 per cent of which are lemons.

Although in a geographically dry area, Iran grows around 3.75 million tons of citrus each year, including threequarters of a million tons of lemons. Much of Iran's citrus is exported to the Middle East and North Africa.

A combination of good weather and fertile soil in the coastal regions lead to Italy producing some 3.6 million tons of citrus per annum. While lemons have long been important in this country, oranges and various species of mandarin have a major stake in the market.

Turkey produces over 3 million tons of citrus per annum, a substantial proportion of which is limes and lemons.

India is the world's largest producer of limes and lemons with approximately 3 million tons per annum.

Nigeria is one of the largest global lemon producers, with a total citrus production of 707,000 tons, much of which is exported.

SWEET ORANGES

Sweet oranges (*citrus sinensis*), including Navels and Valencias, are grown as far afield as Brazil, Florida, California, Arizona, Texas, Spain, Italy, Israel, China and Australia. Jaffas® are found in Israel, Gaza and Spain.

Most oranges are winter season, so in the Northern Hemisphere they become ripe around November and some run through to May or June.

The American fashion for citrus grew in the 19th Century, fostering the export of oranges and lemons from Sicily to the United States, although this was strongly influenced by the Mafia.

With the building of the railroads, improved shipping, advances in irrigation and creative marketing, the citrus industries of California and Florida quickly developed.

California saw the establishment of co-operatives such as the California Fruit Growers Exchange. Excess production resulted in the need to either find a way of storing fruit more successfully or getting people to eat more. Substantial advertising drew attention to the nutritional value of citrus fruit.

In 1907, the Californian Fruit Growers Exchange launched their own brand, Sunkist® - Oranges for health, and the successful slogan "Drink an Orange".

By the 1960s one variety of orange, the Valencia, represented around half of the total Florida and Californian orange crop. Originally imported from Thomas Rivers Nursery of Sawbridgeworth, Hertfordshire, England, in the 1870s, this variety initially became known as Hart's Tardiff in Florida, and Rivers Late in California, until a Spanish grower revealed that it was, in fact, the late Orange of Valencia.

Virtually a universal orange, today the Valencia is grown from the USA to Central and South America, South Africa and Australia, and naturally, it is found in the Spanish province of Valencia. Despite its name, however, some food historians believe that the Valencia orange originates either from Portugal or the Azores, rather than Spain.

KUMQUATS

Kumquats are cultivated in India, Japan, Taiwan, the Philippines and Southeast Asia.

MALTAISE

The Maltaise Sanguine, known as the 'Queen of Oranges', is primarily grown in Tunisia.

SWEET ORANGES FROM FLORIDA

Citrus fruits have been farmed commercially in Florida since the mid-1800s. Today large volumes of oranges are cultivated there, representing an extensive industry that employs many thousands of Floridians, and produces a substantial proportion of the US supply of citrus, as well as major exports to Canada, the UK, France and Japan.

Florida grows many Valencias, a variety which carries ripe fruit at the same time as blossom and new fruit, which therefore cannot be mechanically picked. Hand picking remains the preferred option to harvest these oranges. And it takes time. An average picker needs about an hour to clear an orange tree clean of ripe fruit.

Numerous early varieties of navel orange such as Pineapple, Hamlin, Parson Brown, Washington Navel, Ambersweet and several others have also been grown in small quantities in Florida.

The Pineapple, usually grown on a rough lemon rootstock, has a weak, bright orange skin and is fairly seedy. It needs to be used soon after picking but is rich in flavour and loaded with juice.

The easily peeled Temple oranges are usually considered to be tangors – a hybrid of a sweet orange and a mandarin orange. Originally native to the Orient, their seeds may have been stolen from a little-known sect of Buddhism, but they were named after William Chase Temple, an erstwhile general manager of the Florida Citrus Exchange.

Parson Brown was a Florida clergyman, supplementing his income by growing oranges. The Parson Brown orange is pebble skinned with a light yellow flesh and pale yellow juice.

The Hamlin, named after another Florida grove owner and budded on rough lemon stock, is seedless and smooth skinned and ripens in October, often two weeks ahead of the Parson Brown.

Given that colour is not always an indication of whether an orange is ripe or not, and that some will have an orange skin before they are ripe and turn green again as they ripen, both Hamlins and Parson Browns are usually harvested when ripe but still green.

The fresh orange season in Florida runs from October through to June, with the Valencia harvest beginning in late March through to summer.

Florida has two main areas for citrus cultivation: the Ridge and the Indian River.

THE RIDGE IN FLORIDA

The Ridge is the slightly elevated spine of Florida beginning by Interstate 75 near Leesburg, in Lake County, and running south for roughly 100 miles (160 km) to Sebring. Varying in width from one mile to 25 miles (40 km), it is the Florida Divide.

Florida has from time to time suffered severe freezes – particularly one on the night of 13 December 1962 when parts of the Ridge stayed below -7°C (20°F) for around four and a half hours. Nearly eight billion oranges were lost, and the damage to trees led to the State's production being cut in half.

When freezing air moves into a grove on a calm winter's night, if the sky is clear above, the temperature can be perhaps 3°C (26°F) at ground level and 1°C (34°F) immediately above the tops of the trees. This phenomenon, known as a 'temperature inversion', has led to some groves installing wind machines which, with their large propellers, mix the cold lower air with the warmer upper air above the trees, to avoid the orange crop freezing.

The lakes on the Ridge, and there are many thousands of them, tend to modify the cold air and protect the trees from frost. A cold night in Florida rarely goes below -2°C (28°F), the temperature at which oranges freeze, but it may drop in pockets to -4°C (24°F). Sometimes fires are lit at the edges of the Florida groves to provide a basic form of frost protection.

INDIAN RIVER IN FLORIDA

The Indian River is not a river, but a 121 mile (195 km) long tidal lagoon or estuary running along the east coast between the Florida mainland and the Atlantic beaches. In it, saltwater from the Atlantic Ocean mixes with fresh water from the land and river tributaries. The resulting brackish, slightly salty water is moved more by wind than the tide. The width of the lagoon varies from 0.8 km (half a mile) to eight km (five miles), with an average depth of 122 cm (4 feet).

This body of water provides almost perfect protection for citrus groves. These are located just far enough from the coast to avoid most storms, winds and other damaging weather that never makes it far enough inland to damage the citrus crops. The Indian River region stretches some 322 km (200 miles) south from Daytona to West Palm Beach.

Citrus trees can handle many disparate conditions, but they cannot cope with too much water. While they need plenty of moisture, they will rot and die if their roots are standing in water. As a result, the ground is ploughed into ridges and furrows so that trees are set on raised beds. This allows more root structure to grow above the water table, but Indian River trees are smaller than trees of a similar age on the Ridge, which usually mature at 400–600 cm (15–20 feet) high.

Excess rainwater can run into the furrows and then into ditches in a perimeter canal. Water management is a major concern for the citrus growers of the Indian River, where the water table is often a mere metre (three feet) down.

Sometimes a torrential rainfall will leave the land saturated, and excess water must be drained away, or the trees will rot. But in dry periods water needs to be pumped back into the groves to ensure that the trees have sufficient moisture. Growers set aside an area to form a reservoir, so water is close at hand when needed.

These well-designed groves provide a good habitat for over 150 native species of wildlife, while the trees produce oxygen and absorb carbon dioxide.

The groves benefit from the nutrient-rich ocean silt. This travels up Indian River to be deposited around the citrus trees, helping them to thrive. If storms threaten the groves, growers can flood their land with warm water from the Indian River, raising the temperature to protect the trees and their fruit.

Although the Indian River gives protection from much of any bad weather, it cannot prevent all extremes. In 1895 there was a truly destructive freeze. Starting with a crippling freeze in December 1894, the killer came on the 8th of February 1895 when freezing temperatures went as far south as the Florida Keys.

Tens of thousands of trees were destroyed at the bud union (that is where the rootstock and top part of the tree are joined), and thousands more were killed at ground level. Florida had shipped more than a billion oranges in 1894. The following year this figure was reduced to a mere three per cent of the previous harvest as a result of the freeze.

Lemons are even more sensitive to cold than oranges, and the 1895 freeze killed all of Florida's lemon trees.

The high reputation for first-rate fruit that the Indian River established in the 19th Century has remained strong. By the 1920s the term 'Indian River' instantly conveyed unquestionable quality. Then, in 1941, an official Indian River area was established. This area starts 16 km (10 miles) north of Daytona Beach and runs south through Titusville, Cocoa, Melbourne, Vero Beach, Fort Pierce and Hobe Sound to Palm Beach. It runs about 24 km (15 miles) inland, and more in the south.

Oranges grown in Indian River contain about 25 per cent more sugar than those from the Ridge, and they contain more juice as well. Until the 1960s most Indian River oranges were grown on sour orange rootstock. This rootstock does badly on the Ridge, but well on Indian River soil. Although a tree grown on sour orange rootstock will not produce as much fruit as one on rough lemon rootstock, the tree produces a sweeter and juicier crop.

By the late 1950s, all Indian River groves were within three to five kilometres (two to three miles) of the ocean because a little further inland there were savannahs which were largely under water nine months of the year. In 1959 the Minute Maid® Company built a 3 metre (10 foot) earth wall surrounding 7,000 acres of marsh and pumped out the water. The resulting sandy soil was graded and planted with 600,000 orange trees – an impressive feat that others soon followed.

Since then, Minute Maid® has reclaimed more land including one of the largest lemon groves in the world.

Nearly all the new orange plantings in reclaimed savannahs are grown on rough lemon rootstock. Rough lemon produces a fruit that is virtually all rind and as such inedible, but as lemon rootstock it is strong and vigorous, an ideal base for many varieties of citrus.

These trees grow faster, bear more fruit and are less susceptible to virus-based diseases than they would be on sour orange rootstock. Individual oranges may not be up to the usual Indian River standard, but this does not matter where most oranges are grown for juicing.

In 1990, Florida's Natural® Lemonade made its debut. By 2015 it introduced "Fit & Delicious" its Valencia orange juice beverage with "45 per cent less sugar, 60 calories per serving, no pulp and 100 per cent Florida-grown Valencia taste". (Note the word 'beverage' – this drink is only 50 per cent orange juice and has artificial sweetener in the form of Stevia added.)

FLORIDA ORANGES IN ENGLAND

In the 1770s Londoners developed a craving for Jesse Fish Oranges. 1776 saw Jesse Fish ship an amazing 65,000 oranges to England. These thin skinned oranges were difficult to peel, but incredibly juicy and sweet. And these oranges were preferred for making a drink called 'shrub' – which was a mixture of alcoholic spirits, sugar and the juice of an acid fruit – the original whisky sour.

Fish was a Yankee, a native of New York, and became Florida's first orange baron. Florida had been Spanish for two hundred years and with citrus groves in Spain, there was no need for them to plant commercial groves in the New World in the early days. Instead, the citrus fruit they planted in faraway lands were for medical reasons.

CALIFORNIAN ORANGES

Oranges reached California in the late 18th Century, but the first orchard of any considerable size wasn't planted until 1804 at the San Gabriel Mission. Californian citrus orchards soon became a popular image for promoting the sunshine and easy living of this State.

In California, nearly all lemon trees are grown on orange rootstock.

Californian oranges are light in weight with thick skins. Their flesh is marvellously sweet, and the segments almost separate themselves. California's arid climate results in a thick albedo, or white part of the skin.

Cara cara oranges are wonderfully sweet navels harvested in California between December and April. Their bright orange skins conceal interiors that are juicy and often have a hint of pink – making them perfect for citrus fruit salads. The pigmentation in Cara caras is based on lycopene, not anthocyanins as it is for blood oranges. They have low acid, a tangy bite behind the sweetness, and tend to have very few, if any, seeds.

Cool air comes down most nights in California's San Joaquin Valley. Here growers plant Washington Navel – the most beautiful orange grown in quantity in the US, with a deep flaring cadmium skin and a perfect ellipsoid shape.

The Valencia is a spring and summer orange while the Washington Navel ripens in autumn and winter. The two varieties overlap, giving California a continuous supply.

CARIBBEAN ORANGES

Caribbean islands cultivate and sell a wide range of oranges locally, often with half a dozen types available in a supermarket.

In Trinidad and Tobago oranges are sold on street corners, cut in half and sprinkled with salt. The Jamaican orange sold in Barbados is green skinned. And in Jamaica oranges are cut in half and then used to clean the floor.

SOUR ORANGES

A native of Southeast Asia, and the South Sea Islands, especially Fiji, Samoa and Guam, the sour orange was brought by Arabs to the Middle East in the 9th Century, and was recorded as growing in Sicily in 1002 AD. By the end of the 12th Century it was being cultivated around Seville, Spain.

Taken to the New World, the sour orange was naturalised in Mexico by 1568 and Brazil by 1587, and the Caribbean after that. Spaniards introduced sour oranges to St Augustine, Florida in the 18th Century. Today sour oranges are cultivated wherever there is a commercial market for them, including Southern Europe, especially the province of Seville in Spain, and South Africa (for marmalade), Egypt and the Middle East (for flavouring), India, the Caribbean, Brazil and Paraguay.

Commercial production of the sour Bergamot orange is centred on the Ionian Sea's coastal areas in the province of Reggio di Calabria, Italy, (right in the far south on the 'toe' of the 'boot' of Italy.) The fruit is also grown in Argentina, Brazil, Algeria, the Ivory Coast, Morocco, Tunisia, Turkey and Southeast Asia.

BLOOD ORANGES

Tarocco, Moro and Sanguinello blood oranges are grown in Sicily.

Tarocco trees, along with many other citrus trees, are usually planted in north – south rows, ensuring that the sun falls evenly on their branches to ripen the fruit. These trees are regularly pruned so they don't grow too tall. They also sprout suckers, known locally as *bacchettoni*, from the rootstock, which need to be removed.

The Arancia Rossa di Sicilia (the Red Orange of Sicily) which has Protected Geographical Status, was introduced to the orange groves of Valencia in Spain in the 19th Century, so blood oranges are now coming from Italy, Sicily and Spain.

Spain specialises in blood oranges and Valencias navels, as well as sour or Seville oranges. Blood oranges are expensive in comparison with mass-produced oranges because their season is short and their skins delicate. Supermarkets prefer tougher-skinned varieties such as the Valencias because they cope better with the rough and tumble of supermarket treatment.

MANDARINS

Considered as a native of Southeast Asia and the Philippines, mandarins are abundantly grown in Japan, South China, India, Australia and the West Indies as well as California and Florida. Spain and Turkey are also good sources of this popular fruit.

SATSUMAS

Originating in Japan some 700 years ago, China now dominates the market for cultivating satsumas. In Europe they are grown mainly in Spain followed by Turkey, and in North America today most satsumas are grown in California.

NADORCOTTS

This late maturing Clementine-type mandarin, also known as 'Afourer', originates from Morocco, where it is still grown. It is also found in Spain, Portugal, Argentina and South Africa.

KISHUS

Found in southern China and also grown in Japan, the Kishus are definitely an eastern citrus.

TANGORS

Often called Temple Tangors, these grow well in warm, protected valleys, but will be disappointing in cooler areas. Tangors thrive in hot climates, and the heavy, textured soils in parts of Florida as well as the interior, hottest zones of California, and the Caribbean, including Jamaica.

LEMONS

Lemons are grown commercially throughout semi-tropical climates, with India being the largest producer of lemons globally. They are found in Mediterranean regions including Spain, Italy, Morocco, Greece, Turkey, Cyprus, Lebanon and Israel. They are also grown in areas of the world with a similar climate such as Nigeria, Iran, Mexico, China, California, Brazil and Chile.

The earliest true lemon in Europe was recorded in literature in a 10th Century Arabic treatise on farming and was used as an ornamental plant in early Islamic gardens. It was distributed widely throughout the Arab world and the Mediterranean region between 1000 and 1150 AD (CE).

Historically, citrus was grown on the Italian coast as far north as Genoa, the capital of Liguria, the coastal strip between Pisa and Monaco.

The first substantial cultivation of lemons in Europe began in that city in the middle of the 15th Century.

Half an hour's drive from Palermo in Sicily, is the Conca d'Oro or 'Golden Bowl'. Ever since the 15th Century oranges and lemons have been cultivated in this fertile ground.

The citrus boom in Sicily can be traced back to the 18th Century and endured for over 100 years. The cultivation of oranges and lemons on historical terraces in Syracuse has had a profound impact on the local natural landscape.

Today, Italy is famous for its Amalfi and Sicilian lemons, an essential ingredient in the local gastronomy which uses the juice, flesh and peel of these delicious fruit. The territory for the Amalfi lemon extends along the coast of the Bay of Salerno in north west Italy, but much of the commercial production of citrus fruit in Italy today is now limited to the south of the country and to Sicily.

Lemons were introduced to the Americas in 1493 when Christopher Columbus, took lemon seeds and plants on his second voyage on his vessel *Hispaniola*. Spanish conquests throughout the New World helped spread lemon seeds, where at first lemons were mainly used as ornamental plants and medicinally.

LIMES

Although their precise origin is uncertain, wild limes are believed to have first grown in Indonesia or Southeast Asia, and they were then transported to the Mediterranean region and North Africa around 1000 AD (CE). The Kaffir lime, with its rough green peel and citrus and pine notes, is still popular throughout Southeast Asia.

Limes grow well in the tropics and sub-tropics and are found around the globe. India is the largest producer of both limes and lemons.

Other places growing limes are Egypt, across the Mediterranean, the Caribbean and West Indies, Mexico, Brazil, China and the southern United States.

BRITISH LIME TREE

Note: The tree species known in Britain as the lime tree (*Tilia sp.*) which is called a linden tree in other dialects, is a broadleaf temperate plant unrelated to the citrus fruits. Linden trees can live for many hundreds of years. A tincture or tea is made from the leaves of two different linden trees. Winter linden (*Tilia cordata)* is the small-leafed European linden. There is also the *Tilia platyphyllos*, known as the Summer linden. The linden herb has been used historically as a non-narcotic treatment to help with sleep and anxiety and to lower blood pressure. An avenue of lime trees can commonly be found lining the entrance to a country estate in rural England.

GRAPEFRUIT

The most important cultivators of grapefruit globally have traditionally been the USA, South Africa, Israel, China, Turkey, Mexico and India, but the market has changed. These days, China is by far and away the largest producer of grapefruit.

Grapefruit are categorised by flesh colour – either red (or pink) or white varieties. The white flesh variety known as Marsh Seedless was first planted in Florida around

1860 and is one of the most commonly grown species across the globe, but in recent years cultivation in Spain has expanded and shifted almost entirely to the red varieties, probably because of the misconception that red grapefruit are sweeter than white ones. Similarly, Texas concentrates on pink or red species.

SPANISH GRAPEFRUIT

Oranges have been grown in Spain for centuries, but commercial cultivation of grapefruit there only began in the late 1970s and early 1980s. Spain's grapefruit season runs from October to May, and the later the season, the sweeter the fruit.

Spain focuses on Star Ruby and Rio Red. Created in 1970, Star Ruby is a seedless fruit with a fine, smooth skin, juiciness and deep pink flesh. Rio Red is a very juicy fruit, somewhat paler in colour than Star Ruby, and with a slightly thicker skin and perhaps two or three seeds per fruit.

Although cultivated in other regions of Spain where citrus groves are found, the province of Murcia, in the south east, is definitely the centre for growing grapefruit. While orange and lemon trees have long been cultivated there, grapefruit trees have seen considerable expansion in recent years. Today more than half the total annual Iberian grapefruit production comes from this one province.

Nestling between Andalucia, Valencia and the sea, Murcia in the south east corner of Spain, is ideal grapefruit growing country. The semi-arid Mediterranean climate produces a wide range of fruit and vegetables, much of which is transported to Northern Europe.

Commercially Spain is battling with Turkey, Israel and Florida for grapefruit exports to the European Union, but it has several major advantages.

Large differences between day and night-time temperatures or cold winters increase acidity, but as these temperature extremes are not found in Murcia, the locally grown fruit is low in acid. This gives Spain definite leverage over the competition from Israel and Turkey, both of which produce grapefruit that is more acidic.

Murcia's agricultural wealth stems from a combination of a mild to warm climate and irrigation from two rivers, the Segura and the Guadalentin, which both flow down through sloping groves to the Mediterranean. Some trees are planted on the leeward side of slopes, and others on the windward side, expanding the season for maturity.

The local soil is naturally fertile, leading to little need for the use of chemical fertilisers or pesticides. Success is almost guaranteed with a combination of plentiful sun, few temperature extremes and virtually no diseases or frosts.

Each December sees groves heavily laden with bunches of the golden fruit, often concentrated on the underside of the trees, as they extend down almost touching the ground.

Spanish grapefruit is well known for its perfect uniformity of colour and usually blemish-free appearance.

Both Spain's favoured varieties, Star Ruby and Rio Red, were developed by Richard Hensz, a Texas-based researcher, and have a refreshingly sharp acidity tempered by the fruit's sweetness. Rio Red trees first appeared in 1976 and will typically produce fruit for 30–40 years or more.

Star Ruby was created in 1970 and is a seedless fruit with a fine, smooth skin, and juicy, deep pink flesh. Star Ruby is more widely known than Rio Red, but can be somewhat delicate, with less resistance to sun exposure after several years and lower yields.

Despite these large Iberian crops, grapefruit are only eaten by a relatively small proportion of Spaniards. A survey in 2010 showed a little more than 16 per cent ate grapefruit, and only 24 per cent recognised Spain as a producer. While some 20 per cent of production was going to the home market, most of this was in sales to hotels and cruise ships catering for tourists and foreigners.

Spain has a positive advantage over its competition with its shorter shipping times throughout Europe, giving incomparable freshness. Murcian fruit can be picked in the morning, washed with neutral soap and water, and coated with a thin layer of wax, which falls on the fruit in droplets that are distributed by fans. This protects the peel and helps prevent dehydration.

The grapefruit is checked for quality, size, colour and damage, and then packed by midday and shipped by truck in the afternoon. It will be on some European supermarket shelves the next day, or in the UK within 72 hours.

Competitors such as Israel and Turkey ship by sea, with produce taking 7–10 days to reach its destination. Fruit from Florida, Mexico and South Africa can take a month to arrive, reducing the acidity and leading to an insipid flavour.

AMERICAN GRAPEFRUIT

Several southern States in American are important for growing grapefruit. The season starts in October in Florida and moves west so that the Texan season finishes around May, just as the Californian crops are coming to market, running through to July.

FLORIDA GRAPEFRUIT

Florida's subtropical climate, abundant rainfall and plentiful sunshine falling on its fertile, sandy soil make it an ideal location for growing grapefruit. Much of it is cultivated in the Indian River region. From the ground, the differences between grapefruit and orange trees are not that obvious, but when flying over the Florida groves, the grapefruit trees can be seen to be a lighter green and the orange trees a dark bottle green. The canopies of grapefruit trees are higher than those of orange trees.

For years Florida dominated the international grapefruit market, although its share has declined in recent years, partly because of severe frosts and hurricanes, along with increasing competition – at home from Texas, and overseas from Israel and Turkey.

An added challenge is the industry's struggle with *huanglongbing* (HLB) the 'citrus greening disease', which is devastating to grapefruit, leading to a reduction in acreage. Spending on grove care has had to be increased, making it difficult to grow a grapefruit crop profitably. New grapefruit varieties said to be more HLB tolerant are on the horizon, though proof of their resistance is still awaited.

Traditional varieties from Florida include Ruby Red, Flame, Thompson, Marsh White and Duncan.

The oldest grapefruit variety in the States, Duncan, has a great flavour but is rejected by consumers because it has numerous seeds. The White Marsh is preferred, but for flavour, there is no comparison – the Duncan wins hands down, especially for juicing.

TEXAS GRAPEFRUIT

In the 1960s and 1970s, the Texas-based researcher, Richard Hensz, carefully culled and tested dozens of grapefruit mutations in his laboratory at the Citrus Center and he unveiled the refreshingly sharp acidity of the Rio Red variety tempered by sweetness in 1976. Rio Red is now found in many countries across the globe.

The Texas season for grapefruit runs from October through to June, and its Rio Red is often considered the world's best grapefruit. Named as the State's official fruit, this grapefruit has become an icon of Texas at its best.

ARIZONA GRAPEFRUIT

Citrus are just one type of fruit grown in this plentiful State. Oro Blanco and pink grapefruit are common varieties found here. Yuma County (in Arizona's south west) is now the largest citrus growing region of the State, while production is declining in Maricopa County. However, the Fort McDowell Yavapai Nation Indian Tribe (north east of Phoenix) is becoming a major citrus producer, growing grapefruit, lemon, tangelo, tangerine and Navel oranges.

CALIFORNIA GRAPEFRUIT

California grapefruit tends to be cultivated in Central Valley and Riverside in the State's south. Star Ruby and Marsh Ruby are key varieties here. May to July are the peak harvesting months. The market has seen a boost in demand from home-based millennials enjoying grapefruit together with an increase in exports to East Asia and South America.

CITRON

The first citron varieties to travel west may well have been large, rough skinned and resembling the greenish-yellow cone of the cedar of Lebanon, thus leading to confusion with the citron being called the 'cedar apple'. As a result, when Carolus Linnaeus classified the genus, including lemons, limes, citrons, oranges, grapefruit and tangerines, they were grouped under a name that means cedar.

Many sources consider that botanists travelling with Alexander the Great's troops through Media (in north west Iran) and Persia named the 'citron' and introduced it to Europe, sometimes calling it the Median apple or Persian apple. In the ancient world, it was the 'Golden Apple' that Paris gave to Aphrodite, thus opening his way to the heart of Helen. There seems to be universal agreement that those Golden Apples were indeed citrus.

XXIV HANDMADE PATCHWORK QUILT
Depicting Paddington Bear with a jar of marmalade

XXV CROWN DUCAL ORANGE TREE TABLEWARE
Porcelain and earthenware manufacturers A G Richardson's Pattern Number A1211, launched in 1925

XXVI WELFARE CONCENTRATED ORANGE JUICE
Given to infants in World War II and the following years
(Photo Crown Copyright)

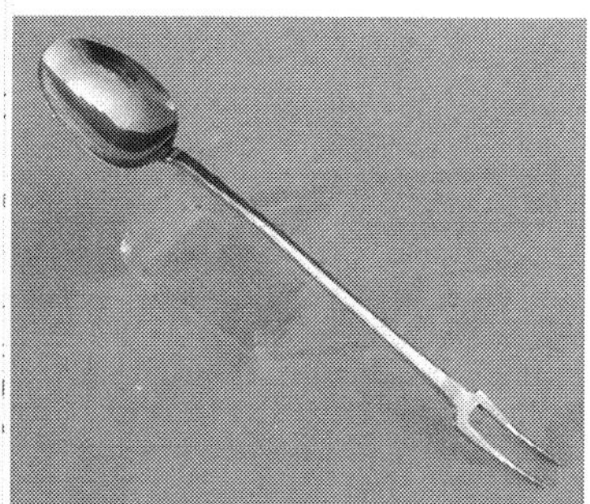

XXVII SUCKET FORK
For eating crystallised fruit
(Photo courtesy Spider Monkey) Spider Monkey are dealers buying and selling antique silverware. For further details go to https://www.antiquesilverspoons.co.uk/about-us.html

XXVIII CRYSTALLISED FRUIT
Used to be a delicious Christmas treat

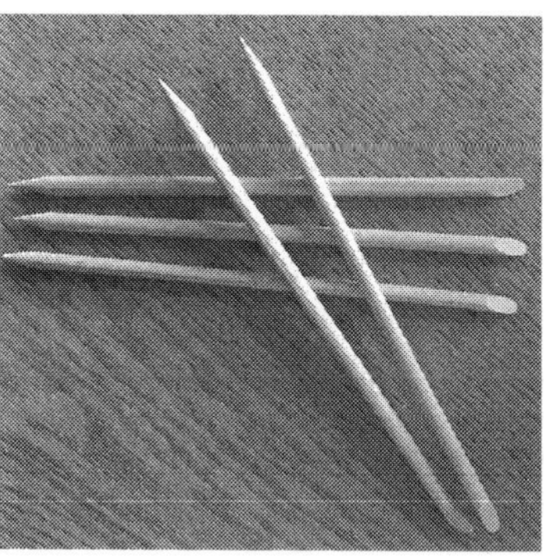

XXIX ORANGE WOOD CUTICLE STICKS
A traditional manicure tool

XXX AMARETTI TINS
Chinotto oranges are used in the making of soft Amaretti biscuits,
a popular Christmas treat

XXXI ORANGE OIL POLISH
Cleans and renews wood, leaving a fresh orange scent
(Photo courtesy Parker & Bailey) Full details of their products from
http://www.parkerbailey.com/natural-orange-oil-polish-16oz/

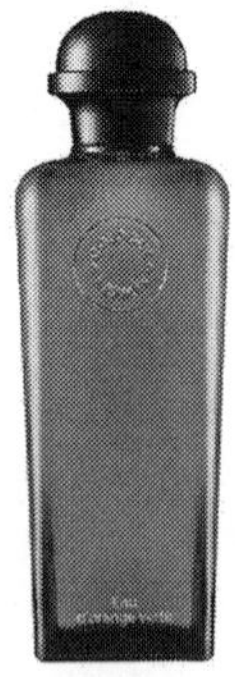

XXXII HERMES EAU D'ORANGE VERTE
(Photo courtesy Hermès Parfums and Studio del Fleurs)
For full range of their products go to:
https://www.hermes.com/uk/en/fragrances/

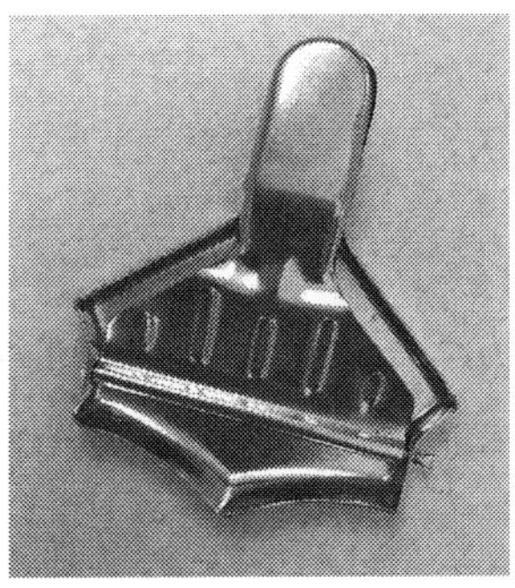

XXXIII INDIVIDUAL LEMON WEDGE SQUEEZER (closed)

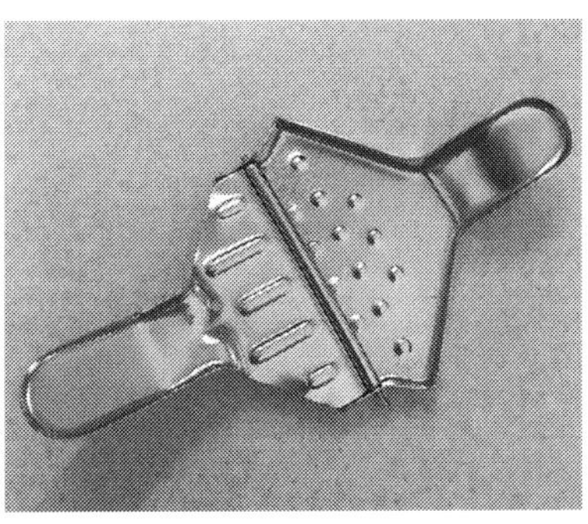

XXXIV INDIVIDUAL LEMON WEDGE SQUEEZER (open)

XXXV BIRD LEMON SQUEEZER
Small lemon squeezer in the form of a bird (closed)

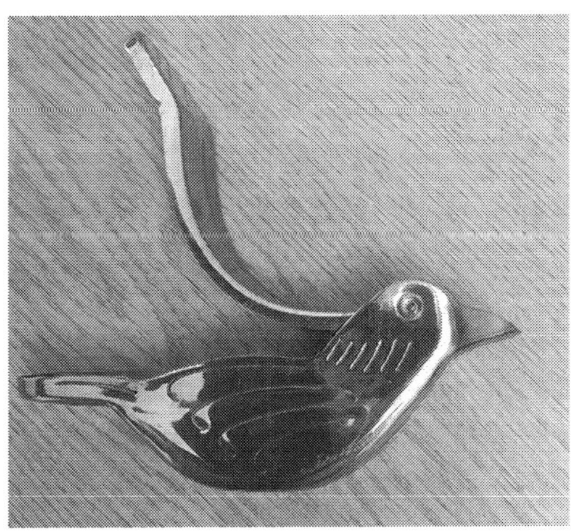

XXXVI BIRD LEMON SQUEEZER
Small lemon squeezer in the form of a bird (open)

XXXVII PLASTIC JUICE EXTRACTOR

XXXVIII GLASS LEMON SQUEEZER (closed)

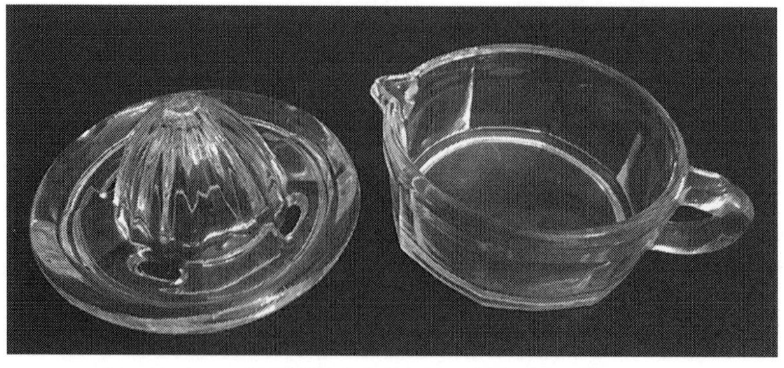

XXXIX GLASS LEMON SQUEEZER (open)

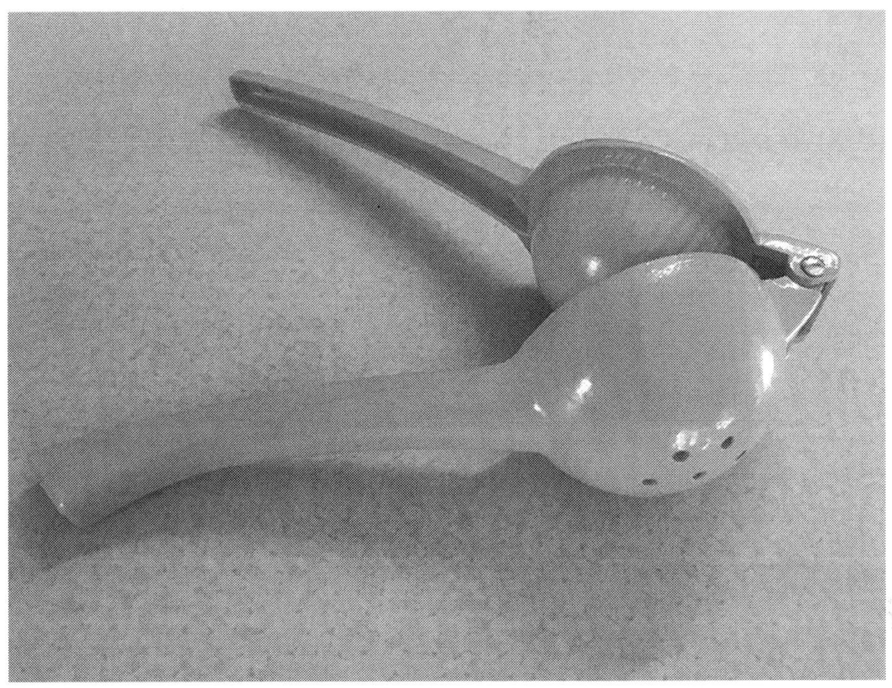

XL LARGE HAND CITRUS SQUEEZER
Easily takes half an orange or lemon

XLI ELECTRIC CITRUS SQUEEZER FOR HOME USE

XLII WOODEN REAMER
A traditional way to extract juice from citrus

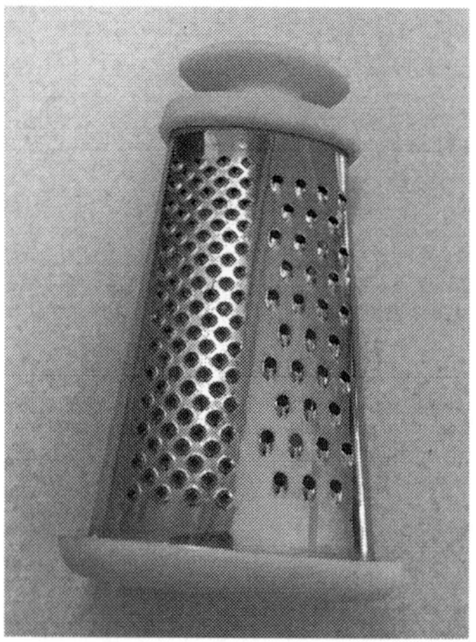

XLIII GRATER
Different sizes of holes in the grater produce varied types of zest

XLIV CITRUS ZESTER

Chapter 6.

THE CULTIVATION OF CITRUS

The word 'fruit' normally relates to the fleshy part of a plant which contains either a seed or seeds. It may be edible or not, and if edible, may be sweet or sour. Fruits account for a substantial percentage of the world's agricultural output.

Botanically, the fruit of any citrus tree is called a *hesperidium*, a special type of modified berry covered with a rind which originated as a thickening of the ovary wall. Citrus is *monoecious*, which means it has both sexes in the same blossom.

Fruits are normally grown in large orchards, and the production of organically grown fruit is expanding with the demand for natural produce. The scientific study and cultivation of fruits is called 'pomology'. As one of the most important fruit families, the cultivation of citrus is a major global industry.

Given that citrus does not grow in cool or cold climates, but prefers semi-tropical or tropical temperatures, there is a 'citrus belt' around the globe. In the north this 'belt' runs approximately from southern China and India, to the Middle East, Israel, Palestine, through to Italy, Spain and North Africa in the Mediterranean, Portugal in Western Europe, then across the Atlantic to Florida, Texas, New Mexico, Arizona and California. Other important areas for growing citrus include Brazil, Uruguay, Argentina, South Africa, Japan and Australia.

Recently, citrus groves have been planted in new countries, such as Swaziland and Cuba, since citrus, and in particular oranges, are seen as big business.

Commercial citrus producers are always looking for improved yield, better storage qualities, attractive appearance and tastier flavours. Some specialists seek the frost-hardy citrus plant with sweet, edible fruit.

'Seedling' is the term used for any citrus tree grown from a planted seed. Seedlings are about 15 years old before they bear fruit. They may well have vicious thorns. However, citrus does not come true to seed.

The introduction of grafting in commercial planting during the mid- and late-19th Century was constructive for the prevention of disease as well as improving the quality of fruit. Citrus have always responded well to human intervention in the form of pruning, budding and grafting.

Most citrus trees consist of two parts, the 'rootstock' and the 'scion'. The rootstock is the lower portion of the trunk and root system, which is mainly underground.

Rootstocks are chosen for their hardiness and resistance to disease. The rootstock also determines the height of the tree, so scions will be grafted onto dwarf, semi-dwarf or standard rootstocks, depending on the desired size of the mature tree.

Trees that would produce poor quality fruit may be valuable for their rootstock. Bitter oranges, like those found in Seville, Spain and used for Scottish marmalade, make the best rootstock in some soils, such as in Florida's Indian River area.

The upper tree, or 'scion', is the part above ground. The scion is selected for its crop and produces the fruit.

The propagation of citrus fruit is usually by budding, although a few varieties can be grown by grafting.

The scion and rootstock are joined at the 'bud union', which is where the bud is grafted onto the rootstock. The rootstock is cut with a short vertical slit a few inches above the ground. A second cut is made so that the flaps of the wound can be lifted and the base of the scion bud can be inserted. This wound is then bound with a bandage, and within a few weeks the new shoot will start growing.

Once it is established, the bandage is removed and any remaining rootstock branches above the join are cut away.

Budwood is the portion of a stem or branch with vegetative buds used for the propagation of new trees. The bud-eye is located at the axis of the leaf and is removed for budding or grafting a new tree. Budded trees bear fruit within five years and are virtually free of thorns.

A single citrus tree can have a number of varied grafts producing oranges, lemons, limes, grapefruit and tangerines, all ripening on different branches of the same tree, often at the same time.

Citrus trees are very cosmopolitan when it comes to soil and seem able to adapt to almost any type. Topsoil, the uppermost layer, usually the top 13 to 25 cm (5 to 10 inches) has the highest concentration of organic matter and micro-organisms.

Citrus will grow in a wide variety of top soils from light sandy through loams to heavy black adobe soils with a high clay content. Adobe soils will swell with rain, and then shrink and crack in dry summer weather. Given a choice, most citrus flourish best in soft, sandy loams.

The subsoil, which is the layer under the topsoil, can influence how well the trees grow more than the topsoil. The subsoil should not be too loose and open, nor should it be so hard and solid that the roots have difficulty penetrating it. It should not be impervious to water, but able to retain some moisture.

It is important to prepare well before planting a citrus grove. The soil should be well ploughed. Any cover crop, that is a crop planted to improve the soil's physical structure and fertility, should be turned under during ploughing.

So that the sun can fall on the trees evenly throughout the day as the earth rotates, citrus are usually be planted in rows running north – south.

When planting saplings, the distance between trees is determined by the variety. The smaller growing varieties such as mandarin oranges and limes, should not normally be more densely planted than 500 trees to the hectare (200 trees per acre). This means trees should be about 3.7–5.5 metres (12–18 feet) apart. Larger growing varieties will be limited to 250 trees per hectare (100 trees per acre), so these trees will be 5.5–7.6 metres (18–25 feet) apart.

Once a citrus grove is planted, ploughing between the trees should take place before the trees come into full bloom, after which only shallow ploughing should be used to avoid cutting the tree roots.

SWEET ORANGES

Sweet oranges grow best in well drained, loamy soil as the plants do not like their roots to be water-logged. They prefer a neutral pH of between 6.5 to 7.5. A dry climate with some 50–75 cm (20–30 inches) of rainfall in the summer months is preferred. A daytime temperature of 20° to 30°C (68–86°F) is ideal with a drop in night-time temperature to ensure that the ripening fruit turn from green to a golden orange.

These evergreen trees can reach a height of around 6 metres (20 feet). Their broad, medium-sized ovate leaves are glossy and their white, fragrant flowers have five petals.

Oranges can set fruit *parthenocarpically* – that is by 'virgin development' – so they can develop a fruit even if the flower is not fertilised. The resulting fruit, however, will be seedless.

SOUR ORANGES

When the Moors invaded Spain in 711 AD and introduced the orange tree to Seville, they brought a tree that produced a bitter orange, whose fruit was not suitable for eating or juicing, but the trees were seen as decorative and provided shade, while the fruit was used exclusively for medical reasons. Later Seville oranges were found in flavourings and in perfume. It was not until the end of the 17th Century that it was used to make a conserve.

The bitter Seville orange grown in Spain is perfect for making marmalade because it has a higher level of pectin (a setting agent) than sweet oranges. Today Spain cultivates around 4,000 tons of these bitter fruit per annum, much of which makes its way to the UK around February each year to become marmalade.

The Seville orange tree is also used as a reliable rootstock.

Various parts of the world use different varieties of sour oranges for flavouring in their cooking. Other bitter oranges such as bergamot are grown in Calabria, Italy, and Chinotto, which is used for crystallised fruit and for flavouring the aperitif Campari, is cultivated in Liguria.

BLOOD ORANGES

Blood oranges bloom early in spring and generally do not fruit in their first growing season. A tree grafted on to rootstock may take three years before fruiting, while a tree grown from seed may take up to 15 years to fruit.

As they can be delicate, blood oranges require a warm climate of 13 to 30°C (55–86°F) and prefer full sun. The soil should be well-drained, so the roots do not stand in water. They must be protected from any frosts, and will benefit from feeding with iron, magnesium and zinc.

MANDARINS

The loose-skinned, sweet flavoured mandarin is one of the hardier citrus fruits and mandarin trees are the most cold-resistant of the citrus trees, although they flourish best when kept frost free.

They prefer full sun, but will grow in partial shade, although they do need well-drained soil with a neutral pH. Trees in full sun produce the sweetest fruit. They are intolerant of waterlogged roots, but only need the minimum of pruning to remove dead or diseased limbs.

Mandarins are perfect for container growing and will usually flourish in a smaller garden or on a sunny balcony or deck.

Their fruit, however, is thin-skinned and small in size, which makes them more susceptible to cold damage than the larger orange and grapefruit. Mandarins grow better when the weather is hot and humid.

LEMONS

Lemon trees are at their best growing between 15 to 30°C, (59–86°F) and once the temperature climbs to 40°C (104°F) it is too hot for them. They do not grow well in the tropics.

Traditionally, Amalfi lemon trees were grown on broad terraces in north west Italy. Each terrace was painstakingly constructed stone by stone and supported by scaffolding made of chestnut posts. In winter the trees were protected from excessive rainfall and hail with a covering of netting hung over these posts.

This labour-intensive cultivation, including the arduous carrying up topsoil and bringing back down sacks of ripe lemons, each weighing 57 kilos (125.5 lbs), is likely to be a thing of the past soon. Low profits and the hard manual labour required to work these steep slopes mean that they are increasingly being abandoned.

Sicilian lemons were often grown on marginal land and steep sites that had been terraced long ago. Such labour-intensive plots were the first to be abandoned, leading to the collapse of dry stone walls and an increase in the likelihood of landslides and erosion. The more lucrative plains around Mount Etna allow for the cultivation of citrus on an industrial scale and are much easier to work.

In the Middle Ages, the lemons that were grown in Southern Italy and Sicily were of a mild or even semi-sweet variety known as *lumia*. Cooks in the north used *verjuice* ('green juice') a highly acidic juice made by pressing unripe or sour grapes, vinegar, quinces or crab apples to create the sour element in food. But as soon as different varieties of quality lemons with a proven consistently bitter taste became available, their juice superseded those previous options. Cooks no longer had to rely on the acidity of sour oranges for the tastes they sought.

The market for lemons and sweet oranges began to expand steadily in the 18th Century. Fruit from the Sicilian Conca d'Oro had always been sold on mainland Italy, but then began to be exported to northern Europe.

None of the crop was wasted. Poor fruit was squeezed for juice to produce citric acid for flavouring and preservatives. And there was a growing market for derivatives such as peel and essences for food and drink. Essential oils extracted from peels also found their way into the perfume industry.

Long famous for its lemons, Sicily's citrus industry passed from one generation to another for centuries. But in recent times it has become vulnerable to both the ever-expanding cultivation of citrus in other countries and the myriad of diseases that can attack the lemon tree.

LIMES

The lime is the most tender of all citrus fruit – its tree is killed by the slightest of frosts but will sometimes sprout again the following year. Plants with fruit called 'limes' have diverse genetic origins, as limes do not form a monophyletic group.

Citrus scientists have difficulty separating the different species and varieties. An example here is the attempt in the early 1950s by the United States Horticultural Station in Orlando, Florida to grow a virus-free Persian lime. This virtually seedless fruit is the one used in everyone's gin and tonic.

The best way to produce a virus-free strain is to plant a seed, but in view of the lack of seeds in Persian limes, researchers cut open more than 1,800 fruit and found no seeds at all.

So they contacted a concentrate plant making limeade and from the pulp of tens of thousands of Persian limes they managed to retrieve 250 seeds which they planted.

Up came bitter oranges, sweet oranges, grapefruit, lemons, tangerines, limequats, citrons – and only two seedlings that turned out to be Persian limes!

Limes like full sun, good soil and a well-drained area to thrive. They tend to have shallow roots, and are happy to have air circulating around any roots that come above the soil surface. A regular supply of water is important, although like most citrus, they do not like to be water-logged. They are more tolerant of too little water rather than too much.

Pruning should be limited to removing dead leaves and branches, trimming any branches that are touching the ground, and cutting back suckers that appear around the trunk.

Insecticidal soap may be needed to protect against attacks from white flies and ants, the key pests for limes. If the trees are in an area where there is the occasional frost, they can be protected with fleece which is generally sufficient, provided the temperature does not drop too low.

GRAPEFRUIT

In the Northern Hemisphere, grapefruit are best planted on south-facing slopes in semi-tropical or tropical regions, and must not be left standing in water or their roots will rot. Winter protection may be needed if the area is subjected to the occasional frost. Only minimal pruning to remove dead or diseased branches is needed.

Grafted trees need a minimum of three years before producing fruit. Any fruit set in the first or second year should be removed to direct the tree's energy into growth for future crops.

The best quality fruit are produced by trees growing in sandy, fertile soils. A mature tree may be 4.5–6 metres (15–20 feet) high and can produce a large crop of 550–700 kilos (1,200–1,500 pounds) per tree.

USA AND FLORIDA CITRUS CULTIVATION

Florida has a subtropical climate, a high rainfall and sandy soil. This soil may be deficient in some components needed for strong growth, so trees may be fed a range of chemicals such as nitrogen, phosphorus, potassium, calcium, magnesium, iron, copper, manganese, zinc, boron and molybdenum. These chemicals are not unusual and are commonly found in the fertilizers in a home garden shed.

Nitrogen, phosphorus and potassium are basic components of many fertilizers. They help plants convert other nutrients into a form that can be used to promote healthy, vigorous growth.

Trees also need a mix of calcium and magnesium – when one goes up, the other can go down – so a balancing act is needed with these two chemicals.

Metallic deficiencies, such as iron, manganese, zinc and copper, can be rectified by supplying them as chelated granules. The word *chelated* comes from the Greek meaning 'craw'. In fertiliser terms, it relates to inorganic molecules enclosed by organic molecules.

ORGANIC AND INORGANIC COMPOUNDS AND CHELATES

An organic compound contains a carbon atom, and often a hydrogen atom to form a hydrocarbon. Inorganic compounds normally do not contain carbon. Organic chemicals will include those compounds found in living things. Inorganics are elemental compounds such as metals and salts.

Inorganic molecules, such as iron, form a loose bond with the surrounding organic chemicals. As well as iron, chelates are useful for applying nutrients such as manganese, zinc and copper.

Citrus is sprayed very little in comparison to some other fruit but chelates can be used in foliar feeding. Many plant leaves have a waxy coating that prevents them from drying out. The wax repels water and inorganic substances, making it difficult for inorganic nutrients to penetrate the leaf. However, when the inorganic fertilizer is sprayed as a chelate, the organic molecules can penetrate the wax, taking the inorganic compound to where it is needed.

Chapter 7.

GENERAL USES OF CITRUS

Citrus fruits have widespread uses and many applications in the home, and historically have been used for centuries. However, nowadays there are many fascinating and some surprising new uses.

CITRUS WASTE

The last decade has seen a dramatic change in attitudes to many waste products. Reappraisal about whether they can be used rather than just discarded has led to some fascinating outcomes.

With world citrus cultivation in 2017 being in excess of 80 million tons, orange juice production and other citrus manufacturing results in large volumes of pulp and peel industrial waste. Until recently this was sent to landfill, but it is now being considered as a rich organic asset.

Citrus by-products, in the form of pulp, peel and pith, are a low-cost resource, but are rich sources of dietary fibre along with Vitamin C, folic acid, potassium, molasses, limonene and pectin.

Costa Rica is a global leader in environmental preservation. A local juice company, Del Oro®, does not use pesticides or insecticides, but produces large amounts of waste citrus pulp and peel. Del Oro® possessed land next to the Guanacaste Conservation Area in the north west of the country. In the late 1990s they arranged that in exchange for signing over the land to the national park, the juice company could dump orange peel and pulp on areas of the land that were seen to have poor quality soil.

Rival juice company TicoFrut® sued Del Oro®, citing the dumping, as dangerous since it created massive piles of rotting peel and flies, with the result that the local Supreme Court ordered the dumping of citrus waste to cease.

Some 15 years later, in 2013, researchers from Princeton University went to Guanacaste and found that the land where about 12,000 metric tons of citrus pulp and peel had been dumped, was thriving. Compared with local areas where no dumping had taken place, the dumped areas had richer soil, greater tree species and more biomass.

According to *Modern Farmer* in 2017 some 3.8 million tons of citrus peel were going to waste each year. A group of Spanish researchers discovered that this so-called waste can be used in wastewater treatment facilities to filter out dangerous metals and other pollutants. Orange and grapefruit peels were first dehydrated and then chemically treated so that the residue could filter out undesirable metals in water.

The fashion industry is also looking at citrus waste. Leading brands like Salvatore Ferragamo are reviewing the use of citrus fibres and fabric. Orange Fiber is an Italian company that has created a textile made by extracting the cellulose from citrus waste while concurrently applying nanotechnology to enrich the fibre with citrus essential oil, which has resulted in a silk-like fabric.

Researchers at the Indian Institute of Technology have developed a way of using the pure citrus extract from orange peel to compress and recycle polystyrene rapidly.

The Orange Peel Exploitation Company (the new OPEC) is an outcome of a collaboration between York University, UK and investors from Spain and Brazil. They comprise an international team of researchers investigating innovative ways to use orange peel waste. Currently, they are looking at using high-powered microwaves to break down orange peel to release valuable gases. These can then be liquefied and used to create oils, cleaning chemicals, plastics and fuels.

The Peel Project is an initiative of the Hong Kong-based industrial design consultancy, Venn Reactor. Starting with the waste from the 700 oranges consumed each month in their office, they wanted to find out what could be achieved with this potential resource. Pooling their skills, they generated and tested a selection of composites, resulting in an assortment of samples with varying properties.

A Peel Project sample from a combination of orange peel and corn starch epoxy produced a mouldable material that feels a little like plastic but possesses sufficient flexibility to prevent it from being brittle. This material was used to create the iconic red Market Lamp seen in Hong Kong's wet markets (that is, fresh produce markets). These lamps are possibly more beautiful than their plastic counterparts, and they have the added advantage of being biodegradable.

Citrus waste can also be converted into natural health products and medicines. Dried rinds are shredded into cattle feed or the sugar in peel is made into molasses for dairy feed, and Italy is one of several places researching how citrus waste can be used as a biofuel.

These are just a few of the diverse ideas about new ways in which citrus waste can become a valuable resource instead of a waste product ending in landfill.

CITRUS FOR HOUSEHOLD USES

Given its ability to cut through grease and act as a gentle bleach, the citrus family makes a great base for household cleansers. The citric acid in lemon powerfully removes dirt and attacks limescale, leaving behind a fresh, clean scent.

As a result, lemon or lime is often found in many commercial washing-up liquids, detergents, kitchen, bathroom and toilet cleaning products.

DEGREASING AGENT

An eco-friendly, all-purpose disinfectant and household cleanser can easily be made at home. Simply collect the peels and skins from any citrus fruits and add to a large lidded bottle of white vinegar. Leave to infuse for at least two weeks; then strain and discard the peel.

The orange or lemon peel provides extra cleaning power as it introduces a fresh aroma to downplay the pungent vinegar smell. The resulting liquid can be used in both the kitchen and bathroom as a safe, natural, degreasing agent to clear away oil and dirt, and instil a light fragrance.

POWDERED GENERAL CLEANER

Dried lemon or grapefruit rinds can be ground into a powder, and then added to baking soda (sodium bicarbonate) to make a great powder cleaner.

REMOVING COFFEE STAINS

Citrus peel, especially lemon peel, works well on coffee stains. Rub a coffee-stained mug with peel and leave to soak. The stain will then be removed in the dishwasher.

REFRESHING MICROWAVE

Put a used lemon in a bowl with a little water in the microwave on high power for a few minutes, giving the water time to boil and the steam to condense inside the microwave. Remove the bowl and wipe the inside of the microwave clean. This will refresh the appliance.

CLEANING THE KETTLE

To clean a kettle, boil thin slices of lemon in the kettle, let it sit for an hour to cool, then pour the water away and rinse well.

SANITISING WASTE DISPOSAL OR DISHWASHER

Put any used pieces of lemon, lime or orange peel after everything else into the waste disposal and run the machine for a clean citrus smell. Citrus popped in as the last thing to be ground in the waste disposal will get rid of nasty odours and leave a clean citrus smell. And a used half a lemon can be tossed into the dishwasher before running it.

CLEANING A WORKTOP

Orange essential oil is both non-toxic and antiseptic, and it works well as a cleaner for tables and kitchen worktops. Use ten drops of oil plus a cup of water in a spray bottle, shaken well and then applied with a clean cloth or piece of kitchen towel to wipe the surfaces down.

POLISHING FURNITURE

Lemon or orange oils are found in several types of furniture polish, sometimes with beeswax added. These polishes clean while nourishing natural wood, leaving a pleasant aroma.

POLISHING METAL

Lemon juice will help remove limescale on taps and bathroom wastes, especially if added to some white vinegar and left to soak. Neat lemon juice can be used to polish copper. But to clean other metals such as brass or aluminium, make a paste of lemon juice with half a teaspoon of baking soda and a teaspoon of cream of tartar.

REMOVING RUST AND MILDEW STAINS

Some rust or mildew stains can be removed from clothes with a mixture of lemon juice and salt. If available, leave in strong sunlight to aid stain removal.

FRESHENING DRAWERS AND CUPBOARDS

Dried orange and lemon peel can be used to freshen drawers. Stud an orange with whole cloves and then hang it in the wardrobe to discourage moths and keep clothes fresh.

MAKING POTPOURRI ESSENCE

Boil citrus peels with cinnamon sticks and then add to a little apple cider to produce a natural air freshener or essence for potpourri.

FURNITURE MAKING

In the past, after bearing fruit for 30–50 years, citrus trees were uprooted and then burned. But there is an environmentally friendly company in South Africa which is recovering these trunks for furniture-making, by hand-crafting each piece. This excellent hardwood is fashioned into beautiful pieces of furniture without any forests being destroyed. It's a truly sustainable product.

MAKING ARCHERY BOWS

Osage orange wood and lemonwood are a couple of the favourite exotic woods used to make archery bows.

MANICURE AND DENTAL USES

Quality orange sticks were used as cuticle pushers and nail buffers were made from orangewood. Originally designed by Dr Sitts, a European podiatrist, they first appeared in 1830.

Orangewood dental points are softwood wedge or cone-shaped points for inter-dental cleansing – although some are made of balsa wood rather than orange wood.

Wooden sticks were the forerunners of modern toothbrushes or dental sticks. In the past, orange twig ends were shredded and used as simple toothbrushes.

TEETH WHITENING – DO NOT USE THIS

Baking soda and lemon juice have been suggested as a mixture for whitening teeth at home – but DO NOT do this. There is no reliable evidence that this works, and the strong acid in lemon juice can harm the teeth's enamel (the outermost layer of a tooth).

BLEACHING HAIR AND CLOTHES

Lemon juice is used as a mild bleach for many things. It can be squeezed onto blonde hair after shampooing. If the weather is good, sitting outside to catch the sun for a few minutes before rinsing with conditioner will add pale highlights.

And a mixture of lemon juice and baking soda forms a gentle bleach in which to soak delicate clothes before hand washing to give them that extra brightness.

REPELLING ANTS AND SLUGS

Citrus peel boiled in water, strained and with a few drops of soap added, makes a garden pesticide that can be sprayed on plants to kill ants and discourage slugs.

REPELLING MOSQUITOES

The oil from orange peel rubbed into the skin will help deter mosquitoes.

REPELLING FLEAS

Limonene, found in lemon skins, is used in the anti-flea treatments for dogs and cats.

DETERRING ANTS

Wipe windowsills with a piece of lemon to discourage ants from coming in.

IMPROVING SOIL

Powdered citrus rinds added to the soil in garden beds will bring in chemicals such as sulphur, calcium and magnesium which help improve plant growth.

DETERRING FELINES

Citrus peels spread around the garden can help to deter the neighbour's cat from using your patch as its litter tray. They hate the smell. Coffee grounds can be added to the peel.

DISSOLVING PAINTS AND VARNISH

A natural solvent and paint thinner can be distilled from citrus peel. This can be used with transparent oil glaze, undercoat, gloss and eggshell paints, and various varnishes. It is also useful for cleaning brushes and tools.

HYDRATING HALF-TIME REFRESHMENT

Orange halves are a healthy and easy-to-eat snack. They are given to players at half time in football matches for a quick burst of energy, and due to their high water content, they help keep the players hydrated.

CHRISTMAS STOCKINGS

Many children will remember having a tangerine put in the toe of their stocking by Santa Claus at Christmas.

TOKENS OF LOVE

Orange blossom has traditionally been associated with betrothal and oranges have long been a symbol of love. Queen Victoria chose to wear a headdress of orange blossom, her only floral adornment, at her marriage to Prince Albert on the 10th of February 1840. Wedding rings in the first half of the 20th Century were often engraved with orange blossom.

In his *Decameron*, a work rich in an understanding of what it means to love and be loved, Italian author Giovanni Boccaccio makes many references to oranges. Lovers wash in orange flower water and a courtesan sprinkles her sheets with orange perfume. Boccaccio writes: “Her chamber was redolent of orange flowers”. In the garden there were the “greenest and lustiest of orange and citron trees (which were) bearing at once old fruits and new and flowers”.

Chapter 8.

SCENTS, FRAGRANCES AND TOILETRIES

With their fresh scent, citrus fruits have a rightful place in perfumes, fragrances and toiletries. Citrus peel is non-toxic, so can be used in home-made toiletries. Care should be taken with essential oils because they can be very powerful and might irritate some people's skin.

NOSTRADAMUS PROPHECIES

French physician, astrologer and prophet Nostradamus published his *Treatise on Cosmetics and Conserves* in 1555 in which he referred to the sensual power of oranges, and included recipes for candied orange peel and marmalade, as well as how to prepare various cosmetics from oranges and orange blossom.

ORIGINAL EAU DE COLOGNE

Giovanni Maria Farina (1685–1766), a native of Piedmont in Northern Italy, came from a family of master distillers of ethanol, the alcohol that is used to carry the fragrance of a perfume. A complex technique, it was first discovered by the Arabs in North Africa but was quickly suppressed because alcohol is prohibited by Islam.

However, the use of ethanol in the production of perfume was well-known by the Farina family as his grandmother came from a long line of perfume makers. From his early teens, Farina took a keen interest in fragrance and became an expert in combining alcohol with fragrances extracted from fruits and flowers.

As a young man, Farina emigrated to Cologne in Germany, where there were strict laws regarding foreign settlers. However, he was granted citizenship. In 1708, at the tender age of 23, he invented a bergamot-based perfume, and in order to show his gratitude to the town, he named his first creation Eau de Cologne, and established what is today the oldest fragrance company in the world.

Farina himself said that: "I have discovered a scent that reminds me of a spring morning in Italy, of mountain narcissus, lemons, grapefruit, bergamot and orange blossom just after the rain. It gives me great refreshment, strengthens my senses and imagination."

Bergamot oil is an essential ingredient, and this was only grown in Calabria, so Farina imported it from his homeland. At first it was shipped in copper vessels, but the oil reacted with the metal, so Farina insisted it was stored in glass. He still experienced problems with the quality, so eventually he took control and imported whole fruit from Calabria, extracting the oil himself.

His subtle fragrance rapidly became famous throughout Europe. In the 18th Century it was an indispensable accessory at many royal courts, and was a favourite of King Louis XV, Napoleon Bonaparte and Mozart. In order to immortalize both the perfume and its creator, Cologne erected a statue of John Maria Farina in the Town Hall tower.

When perfumes were temporarily banned in France during the Revolution, Eau de Cologne survived by being repositioned as a medicinal elixir. Indeed, inhaling a small amount of Eau de Cologne placed in the palm of a hand can give an instant lift.

Other perfume distillers sought to produce their own versions of this fragrance, and in 1803 Wilhelm Mülhens launched a competitive Eau de Cologne. The ingredients of Mülhens' cologne were carefully harmonized bergamot, lemon and orange, providing a uniquely revitalizing effect. Lavender and rosemary are relaxing, and neroli, extracted from the blossom of the bitter orange, provides a calming base note for creating a positive mood.

Farina took Mülhens to court for marketing a similar Eau de Cologne, a battle which lasted for generations, and eventually Mülhens' grandson was forced to select a new name for their fragrance. He chose 4711 from the number assigned to his house in Cologne on the eve of the French Revolution.

For many years Farina and Mülhens were keen rivals, but by the 20th Century 4711 began to outsell the original Eau de Cologne.

The word 'cologne' soon became a generic for referring to a refreshingly light, unisex fragrance with a citrus-based headnote. Today, more than 300 years since its launch, the original Eau de Cologne is still available, with the product exported worldwide.

CITRUS IN OTHER FRAGRANCES AND TOILETRIES

Many a girl will remember being given a yellow lemon-shaped soap enhanced with a refreshing aroma of neroli, the blossom of the bitter orange tree, blended with lemon.

With maturity, she may have moved to Chanel No 5, a traditional citrus perfume favoured by Marilyn Monroe, or Jo Malone's Lime, Basil and Mandarin cologne, or Basil and Neroli. Or she may have encountered mandarin oil which is used to make St Clement's soap.

Bergamot oil is a common fragrance and top note in perfumes. The scent of bergamot essential oil is similar to that of a sweet light orange peel oil with a floral note.

A light, green summer fragrance with bergamot blended with lemon and tangerine, is the aromatic Ô de Lancôme, a citrus, woody cologne with base notes of vetiver, moss and ambergris.

For something more feisty, there is Hermes Eau d'Orange Verte, with its top notes of lemon, mandarin and mint over a base of oakmoss and patchouli.

Acqua Colonia Lemon & Ginger from 4711 is a long-lasting fruity fragrance for both men and women.

For the perfect way to wake up the senses, there are many lemon verbena-based shampoos, foam bath and shower gels, some with added lime for extra zest.

BODY SCRUB

A simple but effective body scrub can easily be made by mixing sea salt or sugar with ground lemon zest and a little olive oil. Rough sea salt or granulated sugar act as an effective, natural exfoliate. As both salt and sugar dissolve in water, these scrubs are ideal for bath or shower use.

HAND EXFOLIATE

Similar to the body scrub above, stir ground lemon zest into olive oil with sea salt or sugar to make a powerful hand exfoliate. Rub hands firmly together with the oil mix and then rinse off the oil with soap.

SIMPLE SOAK

Throw pieces of lemon or orange peel in a warm bath and the citrus oils will scent the water.

NATURAL DEODORANT

The refreshing aroma and disinfectant properties of bergamot oil inhibit the growth of germs that cause body odour, and provide a natural deodorant.

Chapter 9.

EXTRACTS, ESSENTIAL OILS AND ESSENCES

Citrus fruits will provide extracts, essential oils and essences. Extracted from the fruit peels, these products have various and wide-ranging applications, from cooking and medicine to cosmetics and toiletries.

There are major differences between an extract, essence and essential oil. A food ingredient is normally a highly concentrated pure extract, or an imitation essence; the label on the bottle should specify which.

An **extract** is a preparation containing the active ingredient of a substance in concentrated form. Extracts should refer to the natural flavours that have been 'extracted' straight from the source. So a citrus extract has been extracted from the citrus peel, over a period of time capturing the natural, distinctive and rich citrus flavour.

Pure extracts are made by the cold press method, using water, ethyl alcohol, citrus peel and time. The peel is steeped in the liquid for four to six months. After this time, most extracts will be around 35 per cent alcohol. Extracts can be susceptible to light so they should be kept in a dark cupboard, but they do not need to be refrigerated. When using an extract in cooking, especially anything heated, it is best added towards the end of the dish's preparation to retain its potency and flavour.

A flavoured oil, such as orange **essential oil**, is made by squeezing the oil from the peel. These oils are much more concentrated and intense than their extracts, and their flavour is often purer and clearer tasting. Essential oils usually have a shorter shelf life and are less stable. They need to be refrigerated after opening and will eventually turn rancid.

An **essence** is an imitation flavouring. Imitation citrus essences are chemically developed with artificially produced flavouring to mimic the natural taste, but often don't have the complexity of flavours that exist in citrus peel.

For most recipes, the extract is usually the best format to use. The essence will be simply an artificial substitute for the extract, although for an alcohol-free flavour, then essence is the one to use.

Some essential oils are edible, but many essential oils are not prepared for internal use, so are inedible, while extracts and essences, such as liquid lemon extract, are edible. If using an edible essential oil, given that it is more concentrated, only a few drops will be needed instead of a teaspoonful.

Essential oils will give a more pronounced aroma or scent to soaps and toiletries when compared to the extract.

EXTRACTS

An extract is a substance obtained from a plant, drug, or similar via distillation, infusion, etc. often by using a solvent such as water or ethanol. Extracts will contain the source substance characteristic properties in concentrated form and may be sold as tinctures.

Natural extracts are obtained by extracting the essential oils from the blossoms, fruit, roots, and other parts of the plant or the whole plant. There are four main methods used to produce them:

- Expression – when the oil is very plentiful and easily obtained, as in lemon peel.
- Absorption – generally accomplished by steeping in alcohol.
- Maceration – used to create smaller bits of the whole.
- Distillation – used with maceration, but in many cases, it requires expert chemical knowledge and the erection of costly stills.

GRAPEFRUIT SEED EXTRACT

Grapefruit seed extract is a non-toxic antimicrobial acidic liquid derived from the seeds, pulp and pith of grapefruit. It has been found to kill or inhibit the growth of a wide array of potentially harmful bacteria, fungi, viruses and protozoan parasites. It is increasingly being used as an alternative treatment for many infections, allergies and other ailments.

ESSENTIAL OILS

An essential oil is a concentrated hydrophobic liquid containing volatile aroma compounds from plants. (A 'hydrophobic liquid' is one that repels water or fails to mix with water.) Essential oils are also known as volatile oils or ethereal oils.

Essential oils are effectively oils that carry the essence of the ingredient they are cultivated from. They are often extracted by distillation where steam is passed through the raw fruit material leading to vaporisation of the volatile compounds. The vapours are then condensed back to liquid and collected.

A common use of essential oils is to add them to perfumes, cosmetics, soaps, incense, and various household cleaning products.

A popular branch of alternative medicine that incorporates essential oils is aromatherapy in which oils are often diluted and used for massage, diffused in the air, heated over a candle flame, or burned as incense. Some claim that essential oils have medicinal properties.

In some cases, essential oils can be used for culinary purposes, for flavouring food and drinks, but these must be of an edible variety.

ORANGE ESSENTIAL OIL

Orange essential oil is derived from the peels of sweet oranges *(Citrus sinensis),* a variety native to China. It is different from the essential oils procured from bitter oranges, such as Bergamot essential oil which is obtained from *Citrus bergamia.*

This oil is anti-inflammatory, antiseptic, and has many other benefits and uses.

Many positive effects are attributed to orange essential oil. When mixed with a carrier oil and used as a cream or ointment, it nourishes dry, irritated and acne-prone skin. It also may be used effectively for a refreshing treatment of calluses on the feet.

The fragrance released by the oil in the peel helps instil a feeling of happiness and warmth and can contribute to reducing mental anxiety while lowering the pulse rate.

Orange oil can be used as an antiseptic for disinfecting cuts and scrapes, insect bites, boils and other skin eruptions. Its anti-inflammatory properties will aid the reduction of redness and swelling caused by injuries. It also calms the digestive tract while reducing flatulence and acting as a mild diuretic.

At the end of the day, add a few drops of orange oil to the bath water to relax before bedtime. While orange oil provides a mild sedative effect, relieving cramps and muscle spasms, it can keep you alert at the same time.

And it is safe for use with children.

An extraction from the young fruits of Hassaku orange, a Japanese citrus hybrid, has been used medically in skin care treatments for patients with atopic dermatitis.

Two or three drops in a cup of warm water make an excellent facial cleanser, which is especially good for problem complexions.

Anyone with digestive problems can try adding three or four drops to a carrier oil and massaging the abdomen to aid colic or slow digestion.

Half a teaspoon of salt plus five drops of orange oil in a cup of warm water make an effective mouthwash, helping to combat mouth ulcers, bad breath and gingivitis, giving better dental hygiene.

Using its anti-inflammatory properties, a mixture of melted coconut oil and a few drops of orange oil rubbed into painful arthritic joints will help ease pain.

Half a dozen drops of orange oil on a diffuser can boost mood and improve an otherwise 'bad' day.

BERGAMOT ESSENTIAL OIL

Bergamot oil is a cold-pressed essential oil produced from the cells inside the rind of a bergamot orange fruit. The refreshing aroma and disinfectant properties of bergamot oil inhibit the growth of germs causing body odour so it can be used as a deodorant.

Italian women picking bergamot oranges became beautifully tanned, and it was soon obvious that as the oil from the fruit entered their skin, they gained a golden glow.

The chemical 'psoralen' is derived from bergamot oil. Skin protected with sun lotion containing psoralen tans in the sunshine more quickly than untreated skin.

Many will remember the aroma of bergamot on beaches in the latter part of the 20th Century as the oil was used for its tanning properties in some leading sun creams, although it is now known there is a possibility that the topical use of bergamot oil might make skin more susceptible to cancer because it can make skin sensitive to the sun.

Research from 2007, which was led by the Department of Drug Sciences and Products for Health, University of Messina, Italy, suggests that certain components of bergamot essential oil are antibiotic and disinfectant in nature. It has the ability to inhibit the growth of germs, virus, and fungi, and can also effectively prohibit infections, including those of the skin. Bergamot oil is found extensively in skincare soaps and shampoos, and its regular use helps protect the skin from infections as well as encouraging shiny hair.

Bergamot oil stimulates the secretion of certain hormones which lessen the sensitivity of nerves to pain. So it can be beneficial in cases of headaches, sprains, muscle aches or similar symptoms which would otherwise require analgesic pills, thus helping avoid the potential side effects of over-the-counter pain relief medicines.

The School of Health, at the University of Northampton, has demonstrated that bergamot essential oil aids digestion, keeping the gut healthy and lowering the risk of food poisoning. It is also believed it may help cure infections in the colon, intestines, urinary tract, and kidneys.

The flavonoids present in bergamot oil are very good relaxants. They soothe and reduce nervous tension, anxiety, and stress, all of which can help heal disorders such as high blood pressure, insomnia, and depression

LEMON ESSENTIAL OIL

Lemon essential oil is typically used to fight fatigue and insomnia, address conditions such as athlete's foot, warts and acne, and stimulate the immune system. It also works as a mosquito and midge deterrent.

A drop or two of lemon essential oil can be added to a carrier oil and then sprinkled on a cloth and inhaled or added to a bath. But it should not be used without dilution.

LIMONENE ESSENTIAL OIL

Limonene oil from lemon peel may help treat bronchitis and encourage weight loss. Extracts from lemons are found in many over the counter cold and 'flu remedies for their soothing qualities.

LIME ESSENTIAL OIL

Lime essential oil helps prevent infection and heals minor wounds. It offers protection against colds and 'flu, aids digestion and treats acne. It is a veritable powerhouse of nutritional benefits, coupled with antibacterial, antiviral and antiseptic qualities.

However, if extracted through cold compression, it can be phototoxic, so care must be taken when using topically. To reduce the risk of skin damage, it should be diluted prior to application and then direct sunlight should be avoided for at least 12 hours.

Lime extracts and lime essential oils are frequently used in perfumes, cleaning products, and aromatherapy

CITRON ESSENTIAL OIL

Citron essential oil can be extracted from both leaves and peel by cold pressing. This lets the oil retain its aroma and nutritional value. It is rich in antioxidants and acts as a natural antibiotic while aiding the digestion and reducing inflammation. It is also used to flavour drinks and food.

ESSENCES

An essence is a flavouring ingredient, mainly used in a number of recipes to give the flavour and/or aroma of the original ingredient. Commonly available citrus essences are orange, lemon, lime and citron.

Imitation essences are chemically created substances that aim to replicate the flavour and/or taste of the original ingredient. These imitation essences usually do not have the delicacy of the natural flavour; however, they provide a close enough alternative that is more convenient than actual ingredients or extracts, especially when the ingredients or extracts are not easily available or are too expensive.

Still, many people find that imitation essences tend to have an artificially produced taste that does not match with the original taste of the ingredient or pure extract. These people recommend using the ingredient, ingredient-paste or pure extract, even though these tend to be quite expensive.

Moreover, at times, imitation essences tend to be weaker than natural extracts. Hence, many people recommend doubling the amount of imitation essence used as opposed to extract.

Chapter 10.

CITRUS HEALTH BENEFITS AND MEDICINAL USES

Citrus such as orange, lime and lemon, are well known as a good source of Vitamin C, so it is hardly surprising that many people reach for them when winter colds are looming. Citrus fruit contain both soluble and insoluble fibre, two important elements of a balanced diet. They also provide a rich supply of potassium which helps reduce the risk of stroke and heart disease.

As they have little or no fat or starch, and few calories, citrus, and especially grapefruit, are often eaten by those who are watching their weight.

Vitamin C, also called 'ascorbic acid', is found in citrus juice and may help the body absorb iron from leafy green vegetables and other iron-rich foods. But excessive consumption of Vitamin C can increase the amount of iron absorbed from food.

And beware of the unrestricted amounts of pectin, found in citrus pith. In some cases, large quantities of pectin can cause stomach cramps, flatulence or diarrhoea.

LEMON JUICE

Drinking fresh lemon juice in warm water first thing in the morning is seen as a way to boost the body's immune system. Its antibacterial properties help fight infections, although the acid can harm teeth by attacking the enamel, so best to rinse the mouth with plain water afterwards.

A longstanding aid to soothe a sore throat and help fight the symptoms of the common cold is a drink made from lemon juice, honey and warm water.

The digestive disorder 'gastroesophageal reflux disorder', affects the ring of muscle between the base of the oesophagus and stomach. It can be triggered by spicy or acidic foods. And lemon juice can be one of these triggers because it can irritate the lining of the oesophagus, so beware.

LIME

Take care with lime juice. While it does have some positive uses, it also has some negatives.

Lime juice has high citric acid content which can dissolve tooth enamel. When this decay progresses into the dentine, (the layer under the enamel) it will usually lead to sensitivity and toothache.

Stomach ulcers, also known as peptic ulcers, are extremely painful and are found in the stomach lining. For decades doctors thought ulcers were caused by stress, spicy food, smoking and other lifestyle habits. But then in 1982 Australian doctors discovered the truth.

The bacteria *Helicobater pylori* can enter the body and live in the digestive tract. For some people they cause no problem. But for others they cause sores or ulcers in the lining of the stomach or upper part of the small intestine when the thick mucus lining gets thinned. Certain antibiotics can kill the bacteria and help ulcers heal.

However, the citric acid in lime can encourage stomach ulcers, or stop existing ulcers from healing properly.

Drinking unpasteurised lime juice during pregnancy may lead to stomach cramps, indigestion or even diarrhoea, so it would be prudent to avoid lime juice during pregnancy.

Most mammals manufacture Vitamin C for themselves, but humans, along with other primates, and surprisingly, guinea pigs, are obliged to consume it. Anyone eating a mixed diet with fresh fruit and vegetables will normally absorb sufficient Vitamin C, but historically sailors on long voyages on a poor diet missed out on this vital element. As a result, they got scurvy.

This potentially fatal illness causes debilitating symptoms such as aching muscles, livid splotches and swollen legs. Putrid and bleeding gums, loose teeth and foul breath follow. Scurvy often killed more men than enemy action and was greatly feared by seamen.

By the beginning of the 16th Century, although the chemistry was not understood, the antiscorbutic value of citrus fruits had been discovered. Sailors noticed that if they ate limes, lemons or oranges during long voyages, they did not go down with scurvy.

As soon as this was appreciated, supplies of citrus were carried on ships so sailors could consume the fruit during voyages, thus voiding scurvy. Those who already had scurvy, ate citrus and their symptoms disappeared. Their breath was sweeter, their gums stopped bleeding and their strength returned.

So the British Admiralty issued orders for regular rations of lime juice on all of His Majesty's ships, leading to British sailors becoming known as 'limeys'.

Initially the Admiralty sought to keep the use of citrus for seamen a closely guarded military secret, as scurvy was a common scourge of various national navies, and the ability of sailors to remain at sea for lengthy periods without contracting the disorder was of huge benefit to a nation.

However, many other countries, including Italy, were already well aware of the value of the addition of lemon or lime juice to the diet of their sailors.

Then in 1747, James Lind conducted a controlled experiment with seamen suffering from scurvy by which he proved that those given citrus would recover from this illness, although he did not know about Vitamin C or why citrus helped.

To ensure adequate supplies of lemon or lime overseas, Portuguese sailors took citrus trees to St Helena where they were planted to provide replenishment on long voyages. And subsequently Portuguese, Spanish and Arab sailors planted similar citrus stations in Madeira, the Azores and West Africa. The Dutch established citrus groves in South Africa in 1654.

Sulphites are a group of sulphur-based inorganic salts which occur naturally but are also added to food products as preservatives to help extend the shelf-life and hinder the growth of bacteria. Lime juice contains sulphites, and since some individuals are sensitive to sulphite, lime juice can trigger complications such as itchy skin, hives, rashes, stomach cramps, nausea or coughs in some people.

People suffering from kidney ailments should not consume lime juice as it might cause renal damage because of its high potassium content.

CITRON

Citron has many properties with long found numerous medical uses. It is rich in Vitamin C, thus helping to boost the natural immune system and reduce the severity of respiratory infection. It also acts as an anti-inflammatory and pain reliever.

The thick white pith is a rich source of pectin, which was thought to help combat diarrhoea, although this is now being questioned.

Citron oil is used to treat coughs, vomiting, flatulence and also help alleviate seasickness.

GRAPEFRUIT

Research shows that eating grapefruit can be good for health, as they have a positive effect on lowering blood lipid levels, including triglycerides. They contain antioxidants, especially the red varieties. Grapefruit are approximately 90 per cent water, so help to maintain body hydration. And they are also good for the immune system.

Grapefruit juice can lower blood pressure because it interferes with the metabolism of calcium channel blockers. But people taking the cholesterol-lowering drugs statins should take medical advice.

They may need to avoid grapefruit while taking statins because the juice contains a chemical that affects the body's ability to break down or metabolize certain statin medications. When statin takers drink large amounts of grapefruit juice, the level of statins in their blood can increase, raising the possibility of undesirable side effects.

The pith, the white spongy part of the grapefruit, is edible and full of soluble fibre, vitamins and antioxidants. Yes, it may be bitter, but it can lower the risk of colorectal cancer as well as reducing blood sugar levels. And with few calories and limited sugar, grapefruit are an all-round healthy food.

Chapter 11.

HOW CITRUS ARE EATEN

Citrus fruit are clearly popular, both as whole fruit and for their various components. But before eating an orange or cutting a lemon or lime in half horizontally through the centre, always wash its skin to remove debris so that any dirt or bacteria residing on the surface of the fruit will not be transferred to its interior.

Essentially an orange is a globe of juice sacs sealed in an outer protective peel. Other citrus fruit, such as lemons, grapefruit and limes are also often rich in juice.

Citrus fruits comprise three layers – an exocarp, a mesocarp and an endocarp. The *exocarp*, peel or flavedo, is the outermost layer. The *mesocarp* or spongy middle albedo is often called the pith.

The innermost layer, the *endocarp* or flesh, is made up of segments, surrounding any seeds. When opened, the stringy segments show the pulp or juice vesicles.

The flesh of some citrus, such as oranges and grapefruit, is eaten as it is, or preserved as jams, marmalade and other forms, taking a reasonably important part in the human diet. Others, like limes and lemons, are usually just too tart to eat, so they are used for juice or zest.

While some citrus are eaten raw, others play an important part in different cuisines across the globe. The fruits can be used as pulp and flesh, fresh juice and concentrate, peel, oils and extracts.

Oranges, mandarins, satsumas and similar are usually peeled and then eaten raw. A knife may be needed to peel an orange, but satsumas and mandarins have a loose-fitting glove-like peel which is easily removed by hand.

An orange is usually peeled whole and then eaten in separate segments. With a little practice, the orange can be peeled with one spiral cut to the rind. This way the fruit can be prepared for a packed lunch, the peel replaced and held in situ with a rubber band to keep it moist until it is time to eat.

Peeling an orange only takes a few moments, and yet a couple of years ago marketers sought to sell pre-peeled oranges. These were not a success as they were packaged in plastic. Viral tweets appeared highlighting their packaging as a blatant waste of resources, while the presentation could be seen to label consumers as just too lazy to peel their own fruit.

Grapefruit were for many years cut in half, sprinkled with a little sugar, a glacé cherry added in the centre and eaten as a typical breakfast food or starter. Or they were sprinkled with cinnamon and sugar and popped under the grill to melt the sugar. There were even special pointed spoons for helping extract the flesh. Today grapefruit are often served as a bowl of peeled segments.

Orange, mandarin and grapefruit segments are great additions to a fresh fruit salad, or they can be tossed among lettuce and other green leafed dishes. A quick salad is made of peeled grapefruit with rocket and spring onions (scallions); or grapefruit flesh combined with wedges of avocado, drizzled with rice vinegar for a healthy starter.

Many oranges are juiced, with Brazil being by far and away the largest exporter of orange juice in the world.

Lemon slices are used as a garnish for numerous dishes. Wedges of lemons are often squeezed over fish or meat dishes at the table.

For a sharper taste, lime juice can be used. Slices of lemon or lime are added to iced water, and to many drinks such as the classic gin and tonic.

Peel is an ingredient in recipes for cakes, pastries and similar food, or dipped in chocolate as a sweetmeat. Essences are used as flavourings in numerous recipes.

Apart from these standard ways of eating citrus, here are a couple of curiosities.

Australian school children can have 'morning tea', a small break from their school lessons eaten between breakfast and lunch when they are encouraged to have an orange as a snack. These can be prepared when producing the snack pack at home.

Norwegians eat oranges at Easter, a tradition that dates back to the first imports of oranges a 100 years ago. Skiers stock up on their Vitamin C which is believed to help guard against sunburn, an advantage when the sun reflects brightly off the snow.

English children make orange peel teeth and wedge them over their gums at Halloween.

In the United Kingdom, lemon juice is frequently added to pancakes, especially on Shrove Tuesday.

CRYSTALLISED OR PRESERVED PEEL

The crystallised peels from orange, lemon, lime and citron are used for their flavour in foods, relishes and liqueurs or for adding to novelty bread. Dried fruit can be used as decoration. All crystallised peels have a variety of uses and all taste delicious.

Traditionally, peel is crystallised over a period of several days. The fruit is cut into wedges, the small amount of flesh scooped out. Pieces of peel are placed in a saucepan and covered with plenty of water, and then simmered until translucent, perhaps for an hour.

A sugar syrup is then made and the peel pieces are placed in the syrup, brought to the boil, simmered for 20 minutes and then allowed to cool. The peel is left in the solution overnight. This process of 20 minutes simmering followed by overnight soaking is repeated each day for the next six days.

Then on day seven the mixture is brought back to a temperature of 112°C (235°F), and watched carefully to ensure it does not burn. It is withdrawn from the heat and left to stand overnight. The next day the pieces of peel are removed from the syrup and drained on a cake rack until they are dry.

CANDIED CHOCOLATE PEEL

Candied peel can be eaten as a sweetmeat, dipped in melted chocolate, or cut up and added to a number of dishes. It is also found in fruit cakes, especially those made at Christmas.

SALTED LEMONS

In Morocco, lemons are preserved in jars or barrels of salt. The salt penetrates the peel and rind, softening them, and curing them so that they last almost indefinitely. The preserved lemon is then used in a wide variety of dishes.

Chapter 12.

RECIPES AND UTENSILS FOR CITRUS

The title of this chapter is misleading because, there are no recipes as such. Rather it contains a selective glimpse at a number of citrus dishes that appeal to me, and towards the end it covers some kitchen gadgets designed for citrus.

There are many thousands of recipes for citrus. Some are desserts, while others take advantage of the sour or acidic qualities of citrus to cut into the fat or oil found in some savoury dishes. One such classic 1970s recipe was *duck à l'orange*. Duck is notoriously fatty and the orange juice counteracts this oil.

Orange caviar pearls are small drops of gel full of punchy citrus flavour. Created by using a dropper to add a mixture of juice and agar agar to oil, these tiny spheres can be added to many dishes for extra zest. (See photo of mackerel with orange 'caviar'.)

One of the most common uses of Bergamot essential oil is its inclusion with regular black tea to produce the infusion of Earl Grey.

Lemon pepper is made from dehydrated lemon zest and crushed peppercorns and is delicious with fish or chicken. Similarly, lemon salt is made with ground dried lemon zest and salt.

Lemon juice acts as a short-term preservative for certain foods, such as apples, bananas and avocadoes, that otherwise tend to oxidize and turn brown after being sliced. A squeeze of lime juice onto an avocado makes for a healthy and tasty starter.

Olive or flax oil, together with lemon juice and freshly crushed garlic and pepper make a light and refreshing salad dressing, while lemon wedges are a great salt substitute when served with meals, because of their tartness.

A good way to cook whole sea bream is to cut into the flesh to the backbone, insert slices of lemon and bacon in the cuts and then wrap the fish in foil before baking it gently in the oven.

Lemon juice is used to make lemonade, soft drinks, and cocktails. It is an effective marinade for fish, and in meat, the acid helps breakdown the tough collagen fibres, to tenderise the meat.

Lemon barley water is an old-fashioned soft drink used as a tonic, especially for people who are sick or convalescing. It is made with lemon juice or rind, pearl barley, water and honey. High in calories and fibre content, it should only be drunk in moderation. Many health benefits are claimed for this drink, such as improving digestion, promoting weight loss and enhancing the immune system, but not all these benefits have been verified. Nonetheless, a glass of freshly made lemon barley water will certainly help an invalid.

Original recipes for lemon curd dating from the early 1800s talk of the acid in lemon juice turning cream into curds, which were then separated from the whey using a cheesecloth. This traditional English lemon curd is rarely found nowadays, having been replaced by a sweet preserve.

Modern lemon curd is a quintessential ingredient for afternoon tea on the lawn, along with cucumber sandwiches. Sometimes referred to as lemon cheese, this delightful spread is easy to make, using just lemons, sugar, butter and eggs. Full of gusto, lighter than marmalade and much quicker to make, spread lemon curd on toast for a tasty breakfast treat.

Traditionally lemon curd is used as a filling between two halves of a Victoria sponge cake. It also makes a wonderful addition to lemon mousse, a filling for mini choux pastries or a topping for lemon cheesecake. Make it in small batches because, even in a fridge, it will only keep for a few weeks.

Two traditional English puddings are posset and syllabub, both originally incorporating cream, citrus and alcohol. They are similar except syllabub is usually served cold and posset hot. These two rich desserts are normally packed with lemons, although these may be replaced by Seville oranges in some syllabub recipes.

Posset was initially a dessert or drink made from curdled milk enriched with sugar, lemons and a sherry-type alcohol. In 1620 King Charles I was prescribed posset by his physician as it was often given as a cure for colds and fevers. These drinks were kept warm and made in a special cup similar to a teapot with a low-positioned spout so that the liquid could be drunk from beneath the surface foam. By the mid-18th Century posset tended to be thickened with ground almonds, crushed biscuits or egg yolks in place of the alcohol.

One of the earliest recipes for syllabub dates from 1655. In those early days, it was made with lemons and milk, which curdled with the alcohol. The name *syllabub* means 'bubbling drink', and the best way to produce this frothy dessert was to spray milk straight from the udder (for its natural froth) on to wine – not very hygienic, but certainly traditional. An alcohol-free version of syllabub uses cherry syrups and Seville oranges for flavouring.

A popular herbal tea, with a delightfully refreshing taste, is lemon and ginger.

Lemons are generally sold waxed or coated with food-grade vegetable beeswax or similar to prevent them from drying out once picked or from bruising during shipping. When using citrus zest, it is best to avoid waxed fruit, although the unwaxed varieties can still have chemicals on the surface, if they have been sprayed to prevent dehydration after harvesting.

That slice of lemon served in a bar may well be leeching chemicals into your drink. It is best to wash all fruit thoroughly before using them, skip the lemon slice or go for organic fruit.

Citrus flavouring is added to many things from sweets to cake mixes and soft drinks. Limonene, a chemical found in citrus peel, is used as a flavouring in foods, beverages and chewing gum. Carvone is a synthetic spearmint oil made from citrus peel oil which is used to flavour spearmint gum. Although the recipe for Coca Cola® is kept secret in a bank vault, the Coca Cola® Company is one of the world's largest users of peel oil.

There are many different cakes and sweets that contain either lemons or lemon flavourings. A classic is lemon drizzle cake, a light, zesty lemon sponge with a crunchy lemon topping made from a sugar and lemon juice mix. Then there is lemon fudge which is quick and easy to make with lemon flavor JELL-O® Cook & Serve pudding, readily available online and so moreish.

A sponge cake covered in slices of blood oranges and topped with cardamom and crème anglaise is delicious.

As an ingredient, lime juice is found in many cocktails, often based on gin or rum, such as gin and tonic, the Cuba libre, mojito and Daiquiri. Freshly squeezed lime juice is also considered a key ingredient in margaritas, although sometimes lemon juice is substituted.

Combine freshly squeezed lime juice, evaporated cane juice (which is less processed than white sugar) and either plain or sparkling water to make limeade.

Add an-easy-to-prepare zing to dinner by tossing seasoned cooked brown rice with garden peas, chicken pieces, spring onions (scallions), pumpkin seeds, lime juice and lime zest.

Lime is an ingredient of many cuisines from India, and an integral part of a wide variety of pickles, among others, sweetened or spicy lime pickle, salted pickle, and lime chutney. South Indian cuisine is heavily based on lime. Having either lemon pickle or lime pickle is considered essential with the authentic Sadhya, a collection of many dishes in a nine-course meal typically served on a banana leaf for Onam, the state festival of Kerala, India.

In cooking, lime is valued both for the acidity of its juice and the floral aroma of its zest. It is a common ingredient in authentic Mexican, Vietnamese and Thai dishes. Lime soup is a traditional dish from the Mexican state of Yucatan. It is also used for its pickling properties in ceviche, a marinated raw fish or seafood dish. Some guacamole recipes call for lime juice.

The use of dried limes (called 'black lime' or 'loomi') as a flavouring is typical of Persian and Iraqi cuisine.

Anyone visiting the USA should try the American dessert known as Key lime pie. Originally believed to have come from Key West, Florida, this pie is made with egg yolks and sweetened condensed milk in a pie crust, and flavoured with the characteristic Key lime juice.

Another similar dessert is the very popular European dish, *tarte au citron* (lemon tart) in which a pastry case is filled with a delicious mix of eggs, lemon juice and sugar, stiffened with cream.

Orange juice is mixed with champagne to create a classic Buck's Fizz, and the traditional jug of Sangria in Spain is laced with orange slices bobbing on top.

Several well-known liqueurs have an orange content including Cointreau, Grand Marnier and Drambuie. Curaçao acquires its distinctive taste by marinating the green dried bitter orange peel (*Citrus aurantium var. curassaviensis*) and other botanicals, in alcohol, especially gin.

There are many varieties of squashes and other soft drinks, some still, others carbonated, that use orange, lemon or lime as a base flavour. I am the child of a Guernseyman and remember drinking *Orlem*, a squash that was a mixture of orange and lemon, when on holiday in the Channel Islands in the 1950s.

Recipes that combine chocolate and orange were a flavour marriage waiting to happen.

History has it that Marie-Antoinette was a great chocolate lover, and on cold, dreary days she would call for hot chocolate infused with orange blossom water and sweet almonds.

When she complained about the unpleasant taste of some medicine, the court pharmacist, Sulpice Debauve, created the first crunchy chocolate in history by separating the butter from the cocoa mass, and creating the *pistole*. These pieces of dark chocolate contained up to 99 per cent cocoa, or were flavoured with almond milk, vanilla, black coffee, ginger, Earl Grey or cinnamon to the delight of the wife of King Louis XVI.

More than 200 years later, the Pistoles de Chocolat by Marie Antoinette remain a great classic of the French chocolate factory Debauve & Gallais, and chocolate connoisseurs.

Today there are numerous types of orange flavoured chocolate bars, and then there are pieces of crystallised citrus peel dipped into dark chocolate. A wide range of orange-flavoured chocolate products are available, some of which are Daim Limited Edition Orange, Smarties Mini Eggs, Lindor Milk Orange chocolate, and Lindt and Tesco Orange Chocolate bars.

A simple way to make lemon olive oil is to add two or three teaspoons of lemon zest to a glass jar of extra virgin olive oil. Screw on the lid and leave to stand for a couple of weeks, shaking occasionally. Strain the oil, discarding the zest and the oil will have acquired a delicious lemon flavour.

Soft, brown sugar can so easily end up a solid lump in the jar, but a piece of citrus peel popped in will stop it going hard.

Oranges, lemons and citrons were widely used in the 16th and 17th Century kitchens in Europe. Citron blossoms were eaten in salads or preserved in vinegar to be served with apples or sugar. Orange blossoms were used to make superb scented water. Unripe fruit were made into delicate condiments, and tiny oranges found their way into wreaths for their appearance as well as their fragrance.

To extract more juice from lemons and limes, make sure they are at room temperature, and then roll them on a flat surface or place them in a bowl of warm water for several minutes before cutting in half and juicing.

Juice can be extracted in a variety of ways – either with a manual or electric juicer, a reamer, or the old-fashioned way, squeezing by hand against a fork. While any visible seeds can be removed before juicing, there are bound to be some seeds residing deep in the flesh that are not visible from the surface. Half a lemon may be covered with a piece of muslin to prevent any seeds from falling on to a dish as it is squeezed.

Collections of recipes written in longhand were one of the earliest forms of books. They give a good insight into the diets of the past.

A wide range of specialist cooking utensils has been designed specifically for use when preparing various citrus fruit.

There are several devices to extract citrus juice, from the simple wooden reamer or 'squeezer', to manual and electric juicers. In the past many homes had a two-part glass squeezer and today have an electric juicer to extract the juice of lemons, limes and oranges. A small plastic utensil, reminiscent of an apple corer, can be screwed into an orange or lemon to squeeze the fruit to release its juice.

A zester is very useful and more efficient than a grater for removing the zest or thin strips of peel along with the peel oil. If a recipe calls for lemon or lime zest, be sure to use organically grown fruit, since most conventionally grown fruit are likely to have pesticide residues on their skin.

After washing and drying the lemon or lime, run a zester, paring knife or vegetable peeler over the skin to remove the zest, which is the coloured part of the peel. Take care not to remove too much peel as the white pith underneath is bitter and should not be used. The zest can then be more finely chopped or diced if necessary.

If preparing half a grapefruit, a curved grapefruit knife is helpful for releasing the segments. And then when you come to eat the grapefruit, a pointed grapefruit teaspoon enables you to get each segment out easily.

Small wedges of lemon or lime can be put in an individual hand squeezer for use at the table. (See photos of these either in the form of a bird or a citrus segment.)

When every household regularly made their own marmalade, a marmalade slicer was particularly helpful. This device screws on to the traditional kitchen table, like an old-fashioned mincer. A wooden pusher is used to poke wedges of orange or lemon towards the slicer blade, while the handle is moved back and forth, so the fruit is sliced as it emerges from the front of the cutter before falling onto a plate.

XLV ROBERTSON'S GOLDEN SHRED
Traditional orange marmalade
(Photo courtesy Robertson's / Histon Sweet Spreads Ltd. Further details from https://www.robertsons.co.uk/our-products/golden-shred-marmalade/

XLVI ORANGE AND LEMON EXTRACT
(Photo courtesy Tesco plc)

XLVII LIME PICKLE
Spicy lime pickle from Tesco – a taste of India
(Photo courtesy Tesco plc)

XLVIII JAFFA CAKES
Made with real orange juice
(Photo credit courtesy of United Biscuits (UK) Ltd

XLIX PURE ORANGE JUICE

100% Pure squeezed quality Orange Juice from Iceland highlighting it is "Never from concentrate" (Photo courtesy Iceland Foods)

L TINNED MANDARIN SEGMENTS

Often in a light syrup

LI MANDARIN ORANGE SEGMENTS

Canned in a light syrup

LII ANTIQUE HAND CITRUS SLICER FOR MARMALADE, WITH FRUIT

LIII HAND CITRUS SLICER FOR MARMALADE
For use, this utensil screws to the traditional kitchen table

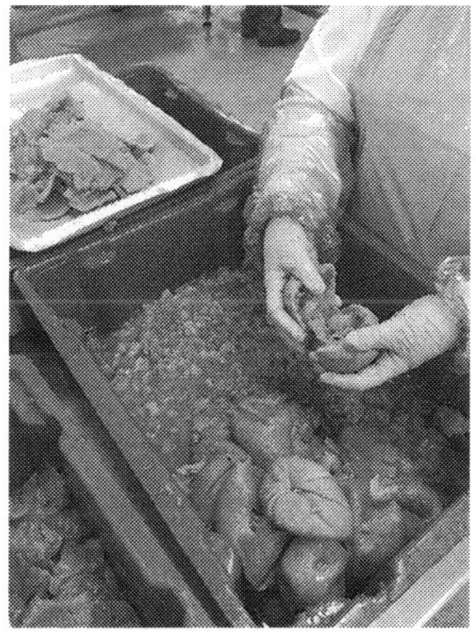

LIV SPLITTING ORANGES FOR MARMALADE
(Photo Credit Wilkins and Sons Ltd. For further details go to:
https://www.tiptree.com/index.php/ourcompany.html)

LV CUTTING GRAPEFRUIT
Using a curved grapefruit knife

LVI GRAPEFRUIT KNIFE

LVII GRAPEFRUIT SPOONS

LVIII HALF GRAPEFRUIT WITH GLACÉ CHERRY
A typical "starter" in the late 20th Century

LIX SELECTION OF ORANGE FLAVOURED CHOCOLATE
(Photo credits: Tesco Zesty Orange Dark Chocolate, image courtesy Tesco plc; Orange Smarties mini eggs, image courtesy Nestlé; Lindt Lindor Milk Orange and Lindt Excellence Orange Intense, images courtesy Lindt - © Chocoladefabriken Lindt & Sprüngli AG; Image of Daim Limited Edition Orange, used courtesy of Mondelez Europe GmbH)

LX LINDT LIME INTENSE
(Photo courtesy Lindt - © Chocoladefabriken Lindt & Sprüngli AG)

LXI LINDT PINK GRAPEFRUIT
(Photo courtesy Lindt - © Chocoladefabriken Lindt & Sprüngli AG)

LXII MOULES ET FRITES
With wedge of lemon

LXIII MACKEREL WITH ORANGE
Mackerel marinated in orange juice, and served with fennel, star anise foam and orange "caviar"

LXIV LEMON WITH OLIVE OIL SHORTBREAD
Shortbread made with olive oil and served with lemon crémeux, lime Chantilly, mini meringues and morsels of lemon ice cream.

LXV HOMEMADE LEMONADE

LXVI LEMON FUDGE
Made with lemon flavor
JELL-O® COOK & SERVE
(Photo courtesy Kraft Foods Group Brands LLC)

LXVII HOMEMADE LEMON CURD

LXVIII GIN AND TONIC
Would not be complete without a slice of lime

LXIX ARNOLFINI PORTRAIT
Jan van Eyck's painting of the Italian merchant and his wife shows oranges by the window, indicating their wealth

Chapter 13.

JUICE – FRESH AND CONCENTRATE

Orange juice can be sold ready-to-drink or as a concentrate. Fresh or pasteurised, it comes in cartons, cans or bottles. The quality of orange juice is determined by a number of factors including how much acid and sugar it contains, along with features such as its flavour, colour, cloud and Vitamin C.

The flavour relates to a complex combination of sensations experienced by taste and smell as well as the texture perceived in the mouth and throat.

Orange juice changes colour throughout the year depending on the varieties that are ripe. It is lighter for an early season orange, deeper for mid-season varieties and darkest for the late season fruit. December sees a cadmium yellow, April a golden marigold, and June a Persian orange.

The ‘cloud’ is the technical term relating to the opaque appearance of orange juice. It is formed by soluble and insoluble compounds released when the juice is extracted. The solid particles are kept in suspension by soluble pectin in the juice. Cloud is an important attribute of citrus juices that contribute to the ‘mouthfeel’.

To maintain the cloud in juice and keep it from settling when processed, enzymes have to be killed by raising the temperature of the juice to nearly 93°C (200°F). This pasteurisation occurs in the concentrate factory.

Quality orange juice should be kept chilled, while cheaper juice can be left at room temperature until opened, although to give the illusion of quality, some cheap orange juices and similar orange flavoured drinks are unnecessarily placed in the chiller cabinet in the supermarket.

Fresh orange juice is a good source of Vitamin C and helps the normal function of the immune system. In addition, Vitamin C contains other important nutrients including folate, potassium (good for controlling blood pressure) and phytonutrients.

Vitamin C allows the body to better use calcium and other nutrients to form bones, teeth, red blood cells and collagen. It aids the absorption of iron, reinforces resistance to infections and acts as an antioxidant, while contributing to the metabolism of proteins.

By far the most popular processed juice in the world, orange juice has become a global commodity, traded on the futures exchanges.

Drinking orange juice at breakfast time is normal in the western world, but not so common in much of the rest of the globe.

According to the National Health Service, most children in the UK consume just three portions of fruit and vegetables each day. Only 16 per cent of school-aged children consume the five or more pieces of fruit and vegetables a day recommended by experts.

A similar situation was found in other countries of the European Union. This led to the creation of a legal and budgetary EU strategy to improve consumption through schools.

The School Fruit, Vegetables and Milk Scheme is the campaign developed by the British Government to boost this European project throughout the country. Among the multiple categories of products included in this plan are freshly squeezed fruit juices.

Orange juice is a fun and easy-to-consume concept for children since they are happy to drink a 150 ml glass of juice, and this counts as one of their daily five portions of fruit and vegetables. And a glass of orange juice helps meet the recommended amounts of Vitamin C that should be consumed by children and adolescents.

When orange juice is made at home it should be consumed fairly quickly because it reacts with air and before long starts to separate, producing a bitter taste and deteriorating. In the case of freshly squeezed juice, the nutritional properties only remain intact for 12 hours after juicing.

In the UK orange juice is sold either with or without pulp – 'with juicy bits' or 'smooth' – to offer consumers a choice. Top quality juice highlights the fact that it is pure, fresh and contains no concentrate or added sugars.

In the USA the history of juice is somewhat different because of the vast distances from the citrus groves to some of the consumers. Orange concentrate became the norm there.

Florida's Natural Growers, a co-operative founded in 1933, invested in machines that extracted juice which led to canned orange juice and later FCOJ (Frozen Concentrated Orange Juice) which was sold all year round.

The Florida Citrus Commission asked a research team in the 1940s to improve the quality of processed orange products, with the aim of providing better juice for the American armed forces during World War II, and to make more efficient use of Florida's orange crop. Work began in 1942 at a laboratory in Lakeland, Florida, provided by the United States Department of Agriculture. During the War concentrate or processed orange juice virtually replaced real fruit juice.

Concentrate was seen to have several key advantages. Frozen concentrate is the same every day – and in that market, consistency was everything. With some of the water removed, concentrate was cheaper and easier to transport. With concentrate, only rotten and split fruit were eliminated, so the rest of the crop was used. In comparison, where oranges were primarily used as whole fruit, up to 40 per cent were rejected at packhouses and dumped in the fields. Relatively few people drank fresh orange juice in the States.

Commercial orange concentrate was developed in Florida and is associated with several key names. Dr Louis Gardner MacDowell is known as the 'patron saint' of concentrate, and Ben Hill Griffin of Frostproof, Florida, who had his own concentrate factory, was probably the last of the great orange barons.

Named Director of Research at the Citrus Commission in 1942, MacDowell was charged with finding new uses for oranges. He did not actually invent or discover concentrate. He found it was easy enough to concentrate orange juice by heating so that the water evaporated. The trouble was that it then had almost no taste. When the water was removed, the flavour went too.

MacDowell set out to master this problem. His new research team invented a way in which by over-concentrating the juice and then adding back a small amount of fresh juice to the concentrate and then freezing it, the flavour of orange juice could be retained. Called the 'cutback process', it led to the expansion of the Florida citrus economy as well as surrounding industries for transporting and warehousing the juice. It also created a more nutritious product by restoring some of the Vitamin C that was lost during the heating.

As the fruit moves along a conveyor, it is first scrubbed with detergent and then rolled into a juicing machine. The juice is separated from the rest – seeds, pulp, peel – and driven through a fine mesh screen.

Specific gravity is used as a clear indication of how much acid and sugar a batch of concentrate contains. The 19th Century German scientist Adolf F W Brix devised a special scale in degrees Brix, to determine the sugar level. Orange juice fresh from oranges is usually around 12° Brix which means there are 12 pounds of sugar for every 100 pounds of water.

The juice, without any pulp or juice vesicles, passes through several stages in the concentrate plant, getting increasingly thicker. As it thickens, it develops a biting aftertaste. By the last stage, the concentrate can be as high as 75° Brix, and is like sticky chewy toffee, and a deep apricot colour. At that stage if it is added to sufficient water to take it back to 12° Brix, it will taste of nothing but sweetened water.

As the picking season progresses, the sugar-acid ratio improves. Pineapple oranges are better than Hamlins, but Valencias are the best. Concentrate plants will keep large drums of out-of-season quality concentrate in cold-storage which they can then blend with in-season mixes to achieve consistency throughout the year.

The super-concentrated juice is taken back down to 45° Brix using fresh orange juice which contains additional flavour essences, orange peel oil and pulp. The main flavouring elements added might be orange oil or D-limonene.

True orange oil is a pure cold-pressed product made just from orange peel. It has a natural orange fragrance and golden colour, and is not refined or processed. As an anti-oxygenate, pure orange oil functions as a stabilising agent and reduces the oxidation process, so products last longer. Peel oil is flammable and is the main flavouring essence put into quality concentrated orange juice with the aim of recovering the flavour of fresh orange juice.

D-limonene is a compound extracted from citrus peel. The peel is boiled in water and the resulting oil (limonene) is distilled in steam at a temperature just below 100°C (212°F). Commonly used as a flavouring or dietary supplement, D-limonene is said to offer a variety of health benefits. While it may have lemon, lime or orange oil in it, D-limonene doesn't have the fragrance of pure orange oil. It can be mixed with other agents to make the concentrate cheaper, which is why it is commonly used.

Florida is second only to Brazil in global orange juice production. More than 90 per cent of America's orange juice is made from Florida-grown oranges. At the height of the concentrate market, in excess of 80 per cent of Florida's citrus was processed into canned, chilled or frozen concentrated juice.

Boiled in a vacuum to high viscosity, separated into its components, reassembled and flavoured, it was then frozen solid. It was sold in small cans and its predominant ingredient was sugar.

In the United States after World War II fresh oranges were seen as somewhat old-fashioned. With the post war baby boom and the rise of the suburban lifestyle, peeling an orange was viewed as tedious and time-consuming.

In less than a generation consumption of fresh oranges dropped by 75 per cent. Concentrate enabled laboratory-controlled levels of acids and sugars which ensured colour and flavour could be uniform. Fresh orange juice is less consistent.

Research conducted by the Florida Citrus Commission found that in the USA the more educated a person became, the more frozen concentrated orange juice they could be expected to buy, which was somewhat counterintuitive.

The Minute Maid® Company was developed by a research organisation in Boston which had been trying to make orange juice crystals during World War II when they decided to switch to building Florida's first concentrate factory. Bing Crosby bought twenty thousand shares in Minute Maid® and began to say mellifluous things on the radio about the Florida company that led to the concentrate boom. Eventually Snow Crop concentrate was taken over by Minute Maid®, and Minute Maid® itself was swallowed up by Coca Cola® in 1960.

Coca-Cola® introduced Minute Maid® chilled juice reconstituted from frozen concentrate in 1973, claiming that their process allowed better blending and the elimination of seasonal variations.

In the US, legislation allowed the addition of up to 10 per cent mandarin juice to improve the colour of orange juice. 'Bits', often from completely different oranges, could be added.

If no additional ingredients, such as sugar and chemical preservatives, were added to a 'from concentrate' juice, it was seen as no worse than a juice that was 'not from concentrate'. Not from concentrate isn't the same thing as fresh, raw juice – it is simply juice that's been pasteurized without being concentrated. No matter what type of juice selected, those that do not contain added sweeteners are likely to be of better quality.

Tropicana® (from Pepsi-Cola®) entered the so-called Orange Juice Wars in the 1980s with their Not From Concentrate (NFC) concept. By then consumers were prepared to pay more for the perceived extra value. NFC juice is pasteurised and 'de-aerated' to prevent oxidization. Sometimes held in tanks for months before being packaged, this juice was often adjusted if it was too sour, pale or watery with the use of orange-derived essences.

By the late 1980s the Florida Citrus Commission was committed to producing only the finest, never-from-concentrate juices. This flash-pasteurised juice was promoted as: “as close to a freshly squeezed taste as possible without home squeezed juice”.

The dawn of the 21st Century saw the growth in demand for natural or organic foods, especially on the east and west coasts of the States and throughout Western Europe. Concentrate is losing favour as there has been a substantial move to fresh orange juice, with juice bars opening and fresh juice on sale in supermarkets.

In recent years quality orange juice, even in cut price supermarkets, is now readily available. Clear labelling highlighting ‘Never from Concentrate’ is today seen as a positive marketing slogan.

Although the market for concentrate is still substantial, the range of juices, their qualities and their prices are now extensive. And there is always the option of juicing at home and drinking the results within minutes.

JUICERS IN SUPERMARKETS

Some supermarkets, particularly in Spain, have an automatic orange juice making machine for consumer use. These juicers enable customers to make their own fresh orange juice on demand.

The machines are loaded at the top with whole oranges. The customer puts a bottle in the holder under the juice spout and presses the start button. As the machine runs, oranges topple down and are sliced in half and then pass over the squeezer to release their juice into the bottle below. It takes about 15-16 oranges to make one litre of orange juice. It’s delicious but needs to be drunk within a day.

Chapter 14.

MARMALADE – AND THAT BEAR!

When marmalade is mentioned, thoughts can turn to a traditional breakfast spread, or memories of children's stories of that wonderful bear from Peru. Although marmalade has taken its place at the British breakfast table for over 300 years, it may soon disappear and be consigned to history.

The much-loved tangy spread is vanishing from the nation's breakfast tables – along with the dining tables themselves as few families now sit with one another for their meals. The way food is eaten is rapidly changing.

Many people no longer comply with the civilised rituals that once held meals – and families – together. Few people have time to sit down over poached eggs, buttered toast and marmalade.

Increasingly, while pensioners may still eat toast and marmalade, younger Britons can find marmalade, with its bracing ripeness and bitter shards of peel and zest, somewhat challenging. Eighty per cent of this traditional spread is sold to consumers aged over 45.

In the modern breakfast marketplace – largely comprising *pain au chocolat*, croissants, smoothies or a shop-made meal – poor marmalade loses out. This traditional spread is now in the shadows, overtaken by the likes of honey and peanut butter.

The origins of this preserve are mysterious, and despite what Britons might think, their claim to have invented it is surprisingly shaky.

The Romans were partial to a gooey fruit preserve, usually made from boiled quinces sweetened by honey, which was known as *marmelo*. The name and its derivations are found across Europe, with the generic words for all jams being 'marmelada' in Greece, 'marmelatta' in Italy, 'mermelada' in Spain. Orange marmalade in Spain is made with naranja amarga (bitter oranges) and appears as 'marmellata di arancia' in Italy.

According to C Anne Wilson's compendious *Book of Marmalade*, the first shipments of a Portuguese version – still made from quinces but flavoured with musk and rosewater – began arriving at the Port of London in the late 15th Century. It was greatly sought after, as the fashionable gentry would serve it as a sweet at the end of a meal rather than as a spread on the morning slice of toast.

At the same time, thousands of miles away, a similar quest to make the perfect marmalade was underway. The Japanese eventually invented one using the citrus fruit, yuzu, which was also popular for dropping into hot baths to ward off colds. It remains a top seller.

There is persuasive evidence that orange marmalade was made in England from Tudor times. A record book compiled in the early 17th Century contains recipes for orange marmalade.

What can be said with some certainty, however, is that the Keillers of Dundee were the first to establish a marmalade factory, and put the spread on the mass market to which it is now struggling to cling.

The word marmalade derives from *marmelo*, the Portuguese for quince. In the 15th Century the Portuguese marmelo quince paste, similar to Spanish *membrillo*, reached Britain.

The story goes that the origins of marmalade as an essential spread to go on toast were 'invented' in 1700, when a storm-damaged Spanish ship, carrying sour Seville oranges, sought refuge in Dundee harbour. The cargo of bitter oranges was sold off cheaply to James Keiller, a down-on-his-luck local merchant, whose wife (or mother, depending on which legend you are reading) turned it into a preserve.

The Keiller family certainly takes credit for being the first to produce this preserve on a commercial basis, but one of the earliest known recipes for a Marmelet of Oranges (similar to today's marmalade) appeared in a book by Eliza Cholmondeley around 1677.

With their high level of the setting agent pectin, Seville oranges are often seen as the best for orange marmalade, but they are only available for a few months each year. Marmalade is not only found on toast. It has a place in a range of recipes such as puddings, tarts, sauces, and even ice cream.

Seville orange juice is an excellent acid for cooking. Cocktails and salad dressings, in particular, can benefit from the greater range of flavour found in sour oranges when compared to lemons or limes. This fruit tends to be small and has a short window of availability starting in late December and ending at the start of February.

Marmalade does not have to be made from oranges. It can equally be made from a wide range of citrus fruit including lemons, limes, citron and grapefruit, or any combination, each type having its own individual characteristic taste. In Australia, desert lime can be used for making marmalade.

Delegates at the annual National Marmalade Festival, held each year in Cumbria, may celebrate all things marmalade, but the real item on the agenda should perhaps be how to save its preferred delicacy from a sticky end.

A good start might be saving the preserve from too many gimmicks. For years, the big marmalade manufacturers have been trying to enhance its image by introducing new flavours, hinting at supposedly aphrodisiac qualities, even repackaging it as 'orange jam'. Product labels have been enhanced with added tasting notes and interesting health claims.

Some examples are definitely over the top. One 'ultra-deluxe' variety launched in 2006 retailed at £1,100 a jar, or £50 a spoonful. This fine cut, Seville orange marmalade had added vintage Dalmore 62 whisky from Whyte & Mackay, a splash of Pol Roger Curée 1996 vintage champagne and was garnished with flakes of 24-carat gold leaf.

Many pensioners will remember collecting tokens with jars of Robertson's marmalade which they could exchange for enamel golliwog badges, when they were children. The golliwog logo was there for almost a century as the emblem of the nation's largest marmalade company but was removed following complaints from anti-racism campaigners. This campaign was so successful that in 2001 they dropped the golliwog and the Robertson's brand ceased to exist, being quietly replaced by Hartley's.

However, it is not all bad news. If marmalade can survive the current battles, it can probably overcome anything. In fact, it is believed that marmalade is poised to cash in on the current revival of traditional British foods, preferably those that are locally made.

Makers of marmalade are hard at work all over the country and hope to spread the love of this special spread right across the world.

Marmalade now comes in numerous categories, including man-made, military, clergy, dark and chunky. Their characteristics are essentially based on essentially the marmalade's set, colour, aroma, presentation and flavour.

The fruit peel may be 'thick cut' giving a chunky structure and strong flavour. When the peel is 'thin cut' the flavour is more subtle and the texture smoother. Dark marmalade has brown sugar or black molasses added. Vintage versions will be left to mature for a richer flavour.

And then, while purists say it should be nothing but citrus fruit and sugar, there is a wide range of flavoured marmalades to which various ingredients, such as Grand Marnier, ginger or whiskey have been added. There is even a version made with Earl Grey tea in place of water.

Globally there is an idea that only British people really understand marmalade, know how to make it, and like the taste of this spread. Certainly, it has been a core part of the British national life for centuries, and nowhere else is it made in such abundance and in so many varieties. Manufacturers now need to market this British staple to a younger audience.

Marmalade is easy to make at home, being a simple mix of citrus and sugar boiled together. Preserving sugar should be used when cooking marmalade or jam. It has larger crystals than granulated sugar, so the crystals do not settle to the bottom of the pot nor rise up to the top as froth. This reduces the risk of burning and the consequent need for stirring. It also allows impurities to rise for easier skimming. Because it minimises scum, it helps in the making of make clearer marmalade, jams and jellies.

Winston Churchill steeled himself for war with it (washed down in the morning with a flute of Pol Roger); D H Lawrence wrote novels on it; Paddington Bear would put nothing else in his sandwiches.

The Romans believed their *marmelo* kept evil spirits away, while Mary Tudor ate it in the belief that it would help her become pregnant. It didn't, and she died childless in 1558.

Celebrity chefs such as Antony Worrall Thompson and Delia Smith recommend it in everything from vinaigrettes to puddings. "It's an acquired taste, but we ought to keep up the tradition of eating it," says Worrall Thompson. "Parents should introduce their children to the joys of marmalade, but they give in if the kids say they don't like it."

The words of the faithful to marmalade need to be heard across the land – or a product that has been a part of British life for so long could become toast.

Chapter 15.

TOP 10 TIPS FOR CITRUS CARE

by Emily Rae of Plants4Presents

(The following article has been supplied by Emily Rae of Plants4Presents as a guide to everyone who would like to grow citrus at home.)

At our nursery in East Sussex, we have one of the largest ranges of citrus trees in the country. We grow everything from little starter plants to mature trees, with a wide selection of different varieties. Because we've been growing these plants for over 10 years, and we have several thousand passing through the nursery each year, we have built up extensive expertise on how best to cultivate them. I would like to pass on this knowledge to you for when you grow your own citrus trees at home. Here is a selection of our top tips for looking after and getting the most out of these gorgeous plants.

i. LIGHT

The first thing is that citrus trees need lots of light. Naturally they grow in places like southern Spain and Italy, Florida and California where the sun shines much of the time. So pick the sunniest place you can find for them. A corner on the patio that catches the sun for much of the day, or a sunny windowsill indoors, is ideal. It's the sunlight shining on the plant that brings the flowers on, and they are one of the few plants that really like direct sunlight on their leaves.

ii. WHEN TO WATER

The second most important thing to remember with citrus trees is that you want to water only when the top of the soil is really dry. And it is best to use rainwater.

Let them dry out properly in between waterings. If you think of the Mediterranean climate, they will have a heavy storm and then it might not rain for quite a while. That's what you are trying to mimic at home. So wait for the top of the soil to be absolutely bone dry to the touch before you next water.

If you are new to citrus fruits, you may find this difficult to gauge. You might not always know by touching the top of the soil whether or not it needs water, so here are some other clues that you can use as well.

Although your plant in a pot might feel slightly damp on the top, it can give you some other clues that it's thirsty. If the leaves are slightly curling on the edges, that is a sure sign that the roots underneath are a little bit dry. If you've got your own tree at home, a good habit to get into is to keep picking the plant up and seeing how much it weighs. If you haven't watered in a while, it will slowly get lighter and lighter – and if you pick it up one day and it feels really light, then that's another great clue that it probably needs a good water.

If you are still not sure whether to water, the last thing you can check is to take the whole root ball gently out of the pot and have a look at the root.

There may be some dark, wet soil at the top, so it feels damp to your fingers, but this can be a little misleading because underneath it may be very dry and lighter in colour. In that case, your plant needs a good water.

At the same time as the temperature drops in autumn and water evaporates more slowly, your citrus tree will no longer be putting on new growth. The amount of water your tree will need will be considerably less in the colder months. In winter, allow the surface to partially dry out before watering, then water thoroughly with rainwater, allowing excess moisture to drain away. Overwatering in winter is one of the most common causes of stress in citrus, so keep them on the dry side.

When you do need to water in winter, as always, water heavily from the top and let the excess water drain away. Don't let your citrus tree stand in water and don't water again until the top of the soil feels dry to the touch.

Twice weekly watering in autumn and springtime is fine, and then in winter this can drop to once every 7–10 days.

Just after you've watered it, because it's full of water, it will obviously feel much heavier.

The next thing to consider is how much water. Many citrus like a heavy watering. Remember the rare but heavy rainfalls in the Mediterranean. So if your plant is in a five-litre pot, that means it will probably need at least one litre or a couple of pints of water. It may seem a lot, but if it needs watering, it needs a good soaking. This is not a 'little and often' scenario.

So take your watering-can and give it a good drink. The water needs to go right the way down to the bottom of the pot. And when you pick the plant up after watering, you should be able to see the water dribbling out of the bottom of the pot.

iii. DRAINAGE

Citrus don't like soggy feet. If you leave them in a puddle of water, you will eventually find the roots rot. Drainage is important, so don't let your plant stand in water.

If you've put your tree outside in the summer and it's raining heavily, then you want to think about either chocking the plant up so the water can drain away, or putting some stones between the tree and the bottom of the pot that it's in, so the plant is able to let the excess water run away and it's not sitting with cold, wet feet.

iv. HARDINESS

Different citrus varieties have different degrees of hardiness, so you do have to bear that in mind. There are some citrus varieties, the more unusual ones, like Yuzus, Finger Limes and Chinottos, which are hardy and will take a temperature of minus 2°C, minus 3°C, or even minus 4°C (30–26°F) quite comfortably.

Other citrus varieties such as Calamondins, Sweet Oranges, Satsumas and Clementines, are definitely not hardy and all need to be kept about 5°C (41°F). They can go outside in good weather, and they will enjoy a summer holiday, but they definitely need to come in as soon as the temperature drops, and to stay indoors during the winter.

The last citrus group is the Lemons. Many people love a lemon tree and are surprised that they will take mild frost. A lemon tree – like Lemon Meyer or Lemon4Seasons – will cope when the temperature goes down to minus 1°C (34°F).

You can wrap the pot with hessian or fleece to extend the season outdoors, or bring it close to the wall of your home to give it a bit of extra protection. When you think it is going to be too cold overnight, it is best to move your tree to a new position for the coming months, rather than try moving it in and out every day.

Citrus trees are not deciduous. One or two leaves may drop and that is not too much of a concern, but more than this and it is likely to be a sign that your tree is unhappy. This is almost always to do with too little or too much water. Other things that can cause leaf drop are sudden or dramatic changes in temperature, underfloor heating, being too near to a radiator or in a draught.

January and February are the toughest months of the year for citrus trees when overcast British skies and short days mean they are surviving on minimal light for weeks on end. Some varieties are tougher than others, but we find even in our greenhouses with maximum light, some will develop a bit of leaf drop at this time of year.

In the middle of winter, the dark, rainy days can lead to some leaf drop even if you are doing everything right. Kaffir Limes, Kumquats and some Lime trees seem most susceptible to this, but once the days start to get longer again, they will pick up and put on new growth. In the meantime, try to ensure they are getting as much direct sunlight on their leaves as possible.

Indoors you don't need a conservatory but just a large window to place your tree or trees beside. Try to choose a place where the temperature is reasonably constant. Most citrus will overwinter well, even in quite warm houses, but if your tree does start to suffer mid-winter, hang on in there – spring is just around the corner.

v. POSITION

When keeping citrus trees inside, it's important to choose the one place with the best light in your home. A nice, sunny windowsill is what we are talking about, away from any radiators, away from draughts and up off any underfloor heating.

Bear in mind the variety you have, so you can put it in the right position for winter, and for most of us that right position in cold weather means indoors and in the brightest place you can find.

Plants can be outdoors in summer from June to late September, depending on the temperature, but make sure they are sheltered from cold winds.

vi. FEEDING

Citrus trees need regular feeding, so we recommend a summer and a winter feed. It's important for any plant in a pot to have some additional feed because there will not be much in the way of nutrients, nor much soil for them to draw goodness from. And citrus trees are particularly greedy plants.

A good citrus feed will have the nitrogen, potassium and phosphorus needed along with trace elements. The trace elements are what help the plants draw up the goodness from the soil, enabling them to make strong, healthy leaves and good fruit. Iron and magnesium are also important elements that the trees need to have the healthiest leaves and the best fruit.

If you find that you haven't been feeding, or that the plant is in a small pot, or you've not been using the right feed, you can often see that the leaves start to come through stripy. The leaves may be slightly deformed, bigger than they should be, or with stripy markings, a clear indication of iron deficiency.

Best to use a balanced citrus feed every other watering, throughout the summer and winter. Just add a little scoop of granules to the water. You will find that keeps your leaves and your tree nice and healthy with deep green, glossy leaves.

vii. MISTING

Misting is something that you often see recommended for citrus trees since they originally come from a climate with high humidity. For most people in a normal environment, your home will be humid enough so that it is not too much of a problem. When we grow plants in the nursery greenhouse, it's quite humid and we don't find the need to do a lot of misting. But there are some exceptions.

If your tree is in blossom, you want to get as many of those flowers to set as possible, and misting at this stage can be useful to increase the number of fruits that set on the tree. It is also particularly important if your home is very dry, you have the central heating on all the time, or you have had problems with getting the fruit to set in the past.

If you've got a plant in flower or in fruit bud, misting just means using plain water in one of those little spray bottles. Spray the leaves in the morning or afternoon - either end of the day - not in the midday sun - so that the water on the leaves raises the humidity. That means the flowers are more likely to set and become fruit, and also the little baby fruit buds are more likely to stay on the tree.

viii. RE-POTTING

If you want your citrus trees to grow on and get bigger year after year, you need to re-pot them once a year in the growing season – that's usually from about the middle of March through to the end of July, when the tree is putting on some strong growth at the top. You want to go up a little bit – one pot size is fine – not too big a jump. Some citrus do like to be in surprisingly small pots.

A good rule of thumb to use as a guide is that when the plant is more than three times the width of the size of the pot at the base, it is time to re-pot it. But don't, for example, jump from a three-litre pot to a five-litre pot or the plant will be floundering. By re-potting one size up in the growing season, you are not giving the plant too much of a shock.

Do use a free-draining compost and also make sure that you have some extra drainage. Put some stones in the bottom of the new pot first to aid the drainage, particularly in the winter, and then put a little loose free draining compost on top of the stones.

Then take your plant out of its old pot. There are likely to be some fine roots at the bottom which mean it's growing nicely, so it should move well into the new soil.

Very gently tease these roots out a little bit so that you can move them into the new soil easily, but don't be too aggressive because citrus roots are quite fine. Then fill up the pot with more free-draining compost.

Quality container compost is readily available in any good garden centre. If you prefer, there is specially formulated citrus compost available. Make sure there is plenty of compost all the way around the edge, so the plant is nicely tucked in.

If you want to keep your plants smaller, then don't re-pot every year. Choose a dwarf variety and only re-pot every couple of years, changing the pot size a maximum of one size up. That will keep the plant a bit smaller and more manageable, particularly if you have a small home and you are bringing it inside for the winter months. In years when you don't re-pot, remove the top 5 cm (2 inches) of old compost in late spring and replace with fresh compost.

Once you have re-potted it and you have it firmed down with the new soil, you need to give it a good watering. Give it plenty of rainwater, again so it is running all the way through to the bottom of the pot. This move is going to give your citrus a really good boost so that the tree grows on and puts out some fresh growth and new leaves.

ix. TREAT EARLY FOR PESTS

Outdoors birds and other insects will help to keep most pests at bay. However, indoors over winter, the warm conditions can become a breeding ground for pests.

Scale, mealybug, red spider mite, aphids and caterpillars all do like citrus trees. The trick is to catch them early. Round brown circles, white sticky fluff, webbing, holes in the leaves or stickiness are all signs of pest attack and should be treated as soon as possible. A soapy washing up liquid solution is normally good enough if the infestation is not too advanced. Spray on to the leaves morning or evening a few times a week until it's cleared.

Alternatively, there is a good plant-based insecticide called SB Plant Invigorator as well as a whole range of natural biological controls.

x. PRUNING

Pruning citrus is really straightforward. You are only looking to give your tree a haircut when you think it needs it. It is not about old wood/new wood – nothing complicated. It is just a question of looking at the tree and thinking '*this tree is getting a bit unruly*'.

For example, if you have a Kaffir Lime, they are well known for being a little bit wonky. They go off in all kinds of different directions, and sometimes you start to see a branch which is shooting off on its own. When you prune, always using sharp secateurs and cut immediately above a leaf node to make a good shape. Aim for a neat "lollipop" for many trees. Just tidy up the plant a little bit.

If you want to let your plant go off in its own direction, you can. It won't do it any harm, and if you like the natural look, that's fine, but if you start to think it needs to be kept a little bit smaller, then you can prune at any time of year. Just trim back to the next leaf node.

You can re-shape your plants by removing overcrowded branches. If they become leggy, they can be pruned back including the leading (tallest) branch, to induce bushier growth. Occasionally, mature plants may produce a number of fast-growing shoots called "water shoots". Cut these out from the bottom or middle portions of the main branches and shorten those arising near the tips of branches.

That's our top ten tips for looking after citrus trees. I hope these will help you to get the very best out of your own citrus trees because they're such rewarding plants – the scented blossom, the tasty fruits and the great variety that are available to grow at home.

AND THEN THE HARVEST

Although citrus don't always follow a strict fruiting season in the UK, they do usually fruit in the winter months.

Lemon Meyers, Limes, Grapefruits, Kumquats and Clementines will naturally drop when they are ripe, but Lemon4Seasons, Calamondins and Chinottos will need to be picked off the tree when they are fully coloured.

Don't forget citrus are not just for your G&T. Try a slice of lemon in hot water for a healthy alternative to tea or coffee, or use sour oranges and kumquats in place of lemons in your favourite recipes.

Packed with Vitamin C, all citrus are brilliant for keeping away winter colds, but if you find them a little sour on their own, put them through a juicer and even the sourest oranges with a bit of fizzy water and honey make a super refreshing and healthy drink – way tastier than wheatgrass!

BACKGROUND TO PLANTS4PRESENTS

My mother and I launched Plants4Presents, a family business, in 2004. We have a wide range of potted plants, some of which are very unusual and exotic, while others are more familiar.

Over the years we have expanded, and today we offer more than 100 different fruiting or flowering plants at any one time, with the selection changing to reflect what is looking best and in season. We currently have around 30 different citrus plants available, many of which will provide edible fruit for years to come.

If you have any questions, do give us a call on local call rate 0845 226 8026 or on 01825 721162 and we'll do our best to advise you.

Emily Rae

Chapter 16.

CITRUS CURIOS

Here are a few citrus curios, mainly focussing on oranges and lemons.

It is claimed that the word orange has no true rhyme. (But it is not the only word like this – think of silver, purple, month, or even dangerous.

Asian cultures are full of symbolism, especially when it comes to Chinese New Year. In China, mandarin oranges signify good luck because the Chinese word for 'mandarin', *kam*, sounds similar to the word for 'gold'. So, having mandarin oranges around the home at New Year is said to bring riches.

In Chinese Feng Shui, orange is seen as a colour of creativity, wealth and power, while being vibrant, happy and eye-catching. Orange also is the Feng Shui colour for emotions, being stimulating and sociable, while at the same time fighting bad moods and helping one feel the joy of life.

Varied meanings are tied up with citrus fruits. In the Baroque age, it was common to symbolise the lineage of a portrait subject from the Dutch ruling dynasty of Orange by including a small fruit-bearing orange tree or some citrus fruit in a painting.

Citrus fruit appear in many classical paintings, often in the form of a still life, with examples from numerous artists including Matisse, Picasso, Gaugin, Cezanne, Degas and van Gogh who were all inspired by oranges and lemons.

In some paintings the citrus is incidental to the main subject, but nonetheless an important feature, possibly with secondary meanings. Citrus fruit can be used to represent the social or moral status of the portrait subjects.

Jan van Eyck's 1434 *Arnolfini Portrait* depicts an Italian merchant and his wife presumably at their home in Bruges. Oranges are placed by the window in this portrait to indicate the wealth of this couple as at the time citrus was expensive in north Europe.

In contrast, Manet's *Bar at the Folies-Bergère*, (1882) displays a bowl of oranges in the foreground, to indicate that he saw the girl in the painting was a prostitute.

New York has changed its name several times. Founded by the Dutch in 1653 as 'New Amsterdam', it was taken by the English in 1664 and renamed 'New York'. Then the Dutch re-took it in 1673 and renamed it 'New Orange' in honour of the Prince of Orange, King William III. Under the Treaty of Westminster in 1674, which ended the Third Anglo-Dutch War, the city was ceded to the English and 'New York' became its permanent name.

Citronella does not come from Citron, but from Lemon Grass (*cymbopogon citratus*).

The flight recorder in aircraft, commonly called 'the black box', is in fact, bright orange to aid its speedy recovery after an accident.

Founded in 1995, the airline easyJet has a bright orange corporate livery.

Contrary to positive feelings being associated with the word 'orange', 'lemon' has a number of negative meanings. A lemon can be a 'worthless thing', or a 'disappointment', or 'booby prize'.

The sourness of lemons naturally suggests an association with experiences that leave a sour taste in the mouth, with the earliest reference found in 1905 where being *handed a lemon* is treated as metaphorically equivalent to being cheated or given a raw deal.

The Oxford English Dictionary's earliest reference showing 'lemon' as something which is bad or undesirable or which fails to meet expectations is dated 1909. There is also a citation dated three years earlier showing its use in the expression *to hand (someone) a lemon* – meaning 'to pass off a sub-standard article as good', or 'to swindle (a person)', or 'to do (someone) down'.

Chapter 17.

ORIGIN OF THE *ORANGES AND LEMONS* NURSERY RHYME

The first published record of the nursery rhyme *Oranges and Lemons* appears to date from 1744 in Tommy Thumb's *Pretty Song Book*. Over the years there have been a number of lyrical variations of the rhyme, but the one at the beginning of this book is the most commonly recited version today. However, it has clearly changed over the years.

In the 1744 Tommy Thumb version, *Shoreditch* is called Fleetditch and the *Great Bell of Bow* is replaced by a reference to St Paul's Cathedral. It is clear that the rhyme refers to money lending, but it also gives an insight into the importance of the churches and their bells.

The spectacularly dark lines at the end: "Here comes the candle to light you to bed, here comes the chopper to chop off your head" probably refers to practices at Newgate Prison. The jail stood on the current site of the Old Bailey, next to St Sepulchre's church (the bells of Old Bailey in the rhyme). The sound of the church's 'great' tenor bell striking at 9 am on a Monday morning would have signalled the start of any hangings due to take place that week. The prisoners on death row were visited the night before by the bellman of St Sepulchre, who held a candle in one hand and rang the execution bell in the other.

APPENDIX A – TABLE OF CITRUS FRUIT

Common Name	Taxonomic Name	Notes / description
Amalfi lemon	*Citrus Sfusato Amalfitano*	Good flavour, intense aroma, sweet and juicy flesh.
Amanatsu	*Citrus natsudaidai*	Yellowish orange in colour, about the size of a grapefruit and oblate in shape. The fruit usually contains 12 segments and about 30 seeds
Arancia Rossa di Sicilia (red orange of Sicily)	*Citrus sinensis* "Blood orange"	Citrus fruit group encompassing Tarocco, Moro and Sanguinello blood orange varieties
Assam lemon	*Citrus limon*	Also known as Nemu Tenga, an important part of Assamese cuisine. A greenish oval fruit with high levels of vitamin C, turning yellow when ripe, used in refreshing drinks and pickles as well as curries.
Avon lemon	*Citrus limon*	First lemons to be grown in Florida. Heavy cropping lemon suitable for frozen concentrate and source of budwood for commercial propagation.
Balady citron (Israel citron)	*Citrus medica*	Grown in Israel and used for Jewish ritual purposes
Bearrs lemon	*Citrus latifolia*	Closely resembles Lisbon lemon (qv).
Berna lemon	*Citrus limon* "Verna"	Second most widely grown lemon in Spain. No or few seeds, juicy flesh. Also called Fino.
Bergamot sour orange	*Citrus bergamia* or *Citrus aurantium var.*	First appeared in southern Italy in 15th Century. Used for its oil, found in some sun crèmes, perfumes and Earl Grey tea, and purported to have numerous health-giving benefits
Bitter orange (Seville orange, sour orange, bigarade orange, marmalade orange)	*Citrus aurantium* L.	A cross between pomelo and mandarin orange. Used to make traditional British marmalade. Widely used in Turkish cuisine. In China fragrant flowers flavour tea, and in Europe flowers are source of neroli oil for perfume manufacture.
Blood orange	*Citrus sinensis*	Distinctive dark red flesh and raspberry flavour, a hybrid of pomelo and mandarin, contains unique antioxidants called anthocyanins, originally from China.

Common Name	Taxonomic Name	Notes / description
Buddha's hand Bushukan fingered citron	*Citrus medica var. sarcodactylis*	Oddly shaped, divided into finger-like segments. Comprises pith and highly scented rind - no flesh. Only the zest is used.
Calamondin calamansi	*Citrus citrofortunella microcarpa*	Cross between mandarin orange and kumquat. Small citrus fruit, smooth, very thin peel which is edible and sweet, sour taste to flesh. Juice is used as a seasoning, and can be used to make marmalade.
Cam sanh	*Citrus reticulata maxima*	Vietnamese for 'terracotta orange' - this is a hybrid from Asia.
Carter navel	*Citrus sinensis*	Californian variety similar to Washington navel. Recommended for home planting.
Chinotto (Myrtle-leaved orange tree)	*Citrus myrtifolia*	Myrtle-leaved orange tree, produces small, bitter or sour fruit, essential Italian flavouring in Campari and carbonated soft drinks, generically called 'chinotto'
Chinotto di Savona	*Citrus aurantium var. amara subvar. Sinensis*	Ugly tree when young but elegant once mature, tiny fruit with pungent skin and flesh, bitter taste.
Citron	*Citrus medica*	One of the original three citrus fruit. Dry, pulpy fruit used to make jams and pickles in south Asia. Medicinal uses, like combating nausea and skin diseases.
Citrus micrantha	*Citrus micrantha*	Wild citrus from papeda group, native to south Philippines, a progenitor species of lime.
Clementine	*Citrus reticulata, Citrus clementina*	Sweet fruit – cross between mandarin orange and sweet orange, but less acid.
Corsican citron	*Citrus medica*	This variety has a non-acidic pulp. Cooked with sugar to produce jam.
Desert lime	*Citrus glauca*	Found in low land sub-tropical rainforest and dry rain forest areas of Queensland and New South Wales, Australia. Early settlers consumers this fruit and retained the trees when clearing land. Commercial uses include boutique marmalade and restaurant dishes.

Common Name	Taxonomic Name	Notes / description
Etrog	*Citrus medica*	Yellow citron used by Jewish people during the week-long holiday of Sukkot, that comes five days after Yom Kippur. Sukkot celebrates the gathering of the harvest and commemorates the miraculous protection God provided for the children of Israel when they left Egypt.
Femminello lemon, Sicilian lemon Siracusa lemon	*Citrus limon*	Leading Italian cultivar, medium sized fruit, rich flavour, highly acidic, very juicy, few seeds, sets fruit throughout the year.
Finger lime (Australian finger lime)	*Citrus australasica*	Finger lime has been recently popularised as a gourmet bush food. Finger lime is thought to have the widest range of colour variation within any citrus species. Tangy flavour, used for pickles and marmalade; dried and used as a spice. From Australia.
Fino lemon (Primofiori, Mesero)	*Citrus limon* L. Burm. f.	Popular Spanish lemon, thin skin, high juice and acid content.
First Lady Anadomikan	*Citrus iyo lyokan*	Similar in appearance to a mandarin.
Florentine citron	*Citrus medica*	A vigorous, thorny plant with large, pointed leaves. Fruit contains a non-acidic pulp.
Genoa lemon	*Citrus limon* L. Burm.f.	Originally from Genoa, Italy, a Eureka-type lemon, (qv) now commercially viable in Argentina and Chile as well.
Golden nugget navel	*Citrus sinensis*	Medium-large, oblong fruit; smooth pale yellowish-orange; flesh crisp and moderately juicy; pronounced tendency to splitting. Old variety. Not commercially available.
Grapefruit, Duncan	*Citrus paradisi* Macfadyen	Oldest USA grapefruit variety, round fruit, smooth light yellow rind, pale yellow flesh, juicy and seedy.
Grapefruit, Flame	*Citrus paradisi* Macfadyen	Dark pink flesh, juicy, very sweet with few seeds.
Grapefruit, Melogold	*Citrus paradisi* Macfadyen	Hybrid of acidless pummelo and Marsh grapefruit, mellow flavour, tender, juicy flesh.

Common Name	Taxonomic Name	Notes / description
Grapefruit, Oro blanco	*Citrus paradisi* Macfadyen	Hybrid of acidless pummelo and white grapefruit, smooth, greenish yellow rind.
Grapefruit, Ray Ruby	*Citrus paradisi* Macfadyen	Commercially available in California, parentage unknown.
Grapefruit, Rio Red	*Citrus paradisi* Macfadyen	Cross between sweet orange and pomelo, sour to semi sweet taste, grows in bunches.
Grapefruit, Rio Star	*Citrus paradisi*	Distinctive sweet taste and juiciness
Grapefruit, Ruby Red	*Citrus paradisi*	Found growing on pink grapefruit tree in 1929.
Grapefruit, Ruby Sweet	*Citrus paradisi*	Portmanteau name for the Ruby Red, Ray Ruby and Star Ruby
Grapefruit, Star Ruby	*Citrus paradisi* Macfadyen	Cross between sweet orange and pomelo, sour to semi sweet taste, grows in bunches.
Grapefruit, Texas Red	*Citrus paradisi*	Named the official fruit of Texas in 1993, grown in southern Texas
Grapefruit, white, Marsh seedless	*Citrus paradisi*	Cross between sweet orange and pomelo, sour to semi sweet taste, grows in bunches.
Greek citron, Etrog	*Citrus medica* – variety *etrog*	Classified as 'etrog' this reflects the variety's major use for the Jewish ritual etrog during Sukkot – a week long holiday five days after Yom Kippur, celebrating harvest.
Hassaku orange Jagada	*Citrus hassaku*	Japanese hybrid similar to an orange in colour but size of a grapefruit. Juicy, tart but with some sweetness.
Hassaku Tanaka	*Citrus hassaku tanaku*	Hybrid of pummelo and mandarin. Medium size. Yellow/orange colour coarsely pebbled and moderately adherent peel, sour in taste, not very juicy, seeded, but stores well.
Hyuganatsu Konatsu Tosakonatsu	*Citrus tamurana*	New summer orange. Grown in Japan. Possibly a chance hybrid between yuzu and pomelo. Light yellow when ripe, juicy and sweet with slight sour taste.

Common Name	Taxonomic Name	Notes / description
Interdonato lemon	*Citrus limon* L. Burm.f.	A lemon citron hybrid originally from Sicily about 1875, thin, smooth, shiny rind, crisp and juicy with high acidic content and slight bitterness, resistant to Mal Secco disease.
Jaffa orange	*Citrus sinensis* Jaffa	Generic name for quality oranges originally from Israel.
Kabosu	*Citrus schaerocarpa*	Popular in Japan, used in cooking, especially with fish. Closely related to yuzu. (qv)
Kaffir lime, Makrut lime	*Citrus hystrix*	Rough green peel with citrus and pine notes. Native to south east Asia and southern China. Fruit and leaves used in south east Asian cuisine. Its rind and crushed leaves emit an intense citrus fragrance. Juice also used in shampoo to kill head lice and as essential oil used in perfume.
Key lime	*Citrus aurantiifolia*	Also known as Mexican lime or West Indian lime. Hybrid of papeda, micrantha and citron. Sweet flavoured, greenish yellow lime. Used to create Key Lime Pie. Most tender of citrus, killed by slight frost, thin skinned.
Kinnow	*Citrus nobilis Citrus deliciosa*	Cross between citrus cultivars of 'King' and 'Willow Leaf'. High seed content. A low seed variety was developed in Pakistan in 2015.
Kishu	*Citrus kinokuni ex Tanaka*	Very small bright orange mandarin, sweet, thin skinned.
Kiyomi (Tangor Kiyomi)	*Citrus unshiu Citrus sinensis*	Hybrid of mandarin and sweet orange, bright orange colour with textured skin, seedless, easy to peel.
Kumquat	*Citrus japonica*	Resembles very small, sweet orange, often used for decoration or preserved. Eaten without peeling as peel is not bitter. Resistant to cold weather. Grown in Japan.

Common Name	Taxonomic Name	Notes / description
Lemon	*Citrus limon*	Originally from a hybrid of bitter orange and citron. Faster growing than orange and will stand more neglect. Sour taste, high citric acid, many uses in food, cleansing and lemon oil, Used in cordials and lemonade.
Lemon Garey's Eureka	*Citrus limon* "Eureka"	Rough textured skinned lemon with short neck and few seeds.
Lemon4Seasons or Eureka lemon	*Citrus limon* "Four Seasons"	Flowers several times a year. Popularly grown as house plant.
Lime – acid	*Citrus aurantiifolia*	Very sharp juice, thin skin, no seeds.
Limequat	*Citrofortunella floridana*	Hybrid of key lime and kumquat, tasty miniature limes, oval greenish yellow fruit with seeds, sweet tasting skin and bitter-sweet pulp.
Lisbon lemon	*Citrus limon*	Thin to medium, smooth skinned quality fruit with high juice content and acidity.
Lunario lemon	*Citrus limon* "Lunario"	Quick growing with few thorns, elongated fruit with sour pulp.
Maltaise demi sanguine blood orange	*Citrus sinensis* (L.) Osbeck	Possibly originally from Corsica, closely associated with Tunisia. Regarded as best sweet orange in world, easily peeled, tender flesh, juicy, particular pleasant sweetness.
Mandarin orange Mandarin Mandarine	*Citrus reticulata*	Popular small, sweet citrus with strong taste and thin, loose peel. Popular in South Africa where called Naartjies. Used in Chinese medicine and Ayurveda to treat digestive and other issues. Symbol of abundance; displayed during Chinese New Year.
Mangshanyegan	*Citrus mangshanensis*	Wild citrus fruit native to Hunan province, China. One of the pure, non-hybrid citrus species.
Mesero lemon (Fino, Primofiori)	*Citrus limon* L. Burm. Fil	Most popular lemon in Spain, good juice and acid content, very thorny tree originally from Murcia.

Common Name	Taxonomic Name	Notes / description
Meyer lemon	*Citrus meyeri*	Cross between lemon and mandarin orange. Named after Frank Nicholas Meyer, American explorer who brought fruit from China to USA in 1908. Found in mid 1940s to carry Citrus tristeza virus so destroyed to protect other citrus.
Meyer lemon - Improved	*Citrus meyeri* "improved"	Launched in 1975 a virus free version. A compact, reliable lemon. Smooth, thin skinned, with slight orange blush, sweet flesh, less acidic than some lemons, used in cooking.
Minneola tangeloa	*Citrus tangelo*	Hybrid of Duncan grapefruit and Dancy mandarin, sometimes marketed as Honeybell. Pronounced neck, smooth red-orange rind easily peeled, rich, juicy flesh, flavour has touch of grapefruit tartness. Must be cross pollinated to assure good fruit set.
Monachello lemon	*Citrus limon* L. Burm.f.	In Italy resistant to Mal Secco disease but poor quality and yield so not grown much
Moro	*Citrus sinensis* "Blood orange"	An Italian blood orange, with dark, sometimes nearly black flesh, bitter taste with raspberry overtones.
Moroccan citron	*Citrus medica*	Used in food, cordials and for medical purposes.
Myrtle-leaved orange tree (Chinotto)	*Citrus myrtifolia*	Small, sour or bitter fruit, essential Italian flavouring agent.
Nadorcott (also known as Tangold or Afourer)	*Citrus reticulata*	Mid- to late-maturing Clementine-type mandarin. Easy to peel, no pips, and great depth of flavour, originally from Morocco
Natsudaidai	*Citrus natsudaadai Hayata*	Hybrid of pummelo and mandarin. Grapefruit sized fruit. With few seeds. Yellow flesh, and quite refreshing. Grown widely in southern Japan. Fruit quality improves with storage.
Navel sweet orange	*Citrus sinensis*	Name comes from miniature fruit at base, seedless, many varieties, very popular orange for eating and juicing, numerous varieties, perhaps the most popular type of orange.

Common Name	Taxonomic Name	Notes / description
Nepali	*Citrus limetta* Risso	Green yellow fruit resembles citron, no seeds, commercially grown in India.
Orange Sweet orange	*Citrus sinensis*	Hybrid of pomelo and mandarin. Numerous varieties, Valencian and navels most popular
Oro blanco	*Citrus grandis C Paradis* *Citrus maxima*	Similar to Sweetie grapefruit, juicy, seedless, very sweet and lacks tartness, golden yellow peel and bitter, thick rind.
Papeda	*Citrus cavaleriei* (Ichang papeda) *Citrus halimii* (mountain citron) *Citrus latipes* (khasi papeda) *Citrus hystrix* (kaffir lime or Mauritius papeda)	Papedas are a group of less palatable, slow growing, hardy citrus native to Asia. Includes some of most tropical and most frost tolerant citrus plants, they are cultivated far less than other citrus but will hybridise with other citrus. This group contains around 15 species.
Perrine (lemonime)	*Citrus limon Lemonime*	A lime and lemon hybrid released in Florida in 1931, but as it died with hard frost, it was replaced by Persian lime.
Persian lime Tahiti lime Bearss lime	*Citrus latifolia*	Hybrid of key lime and lemon. Most cultivated lime species. Larger than Key Lime and less bitter. Seedless and with long shelf life. Bushes have no thorns. Less acidic than Key Lime.
Pomelo, pummelo, pamplemousse, Shaddock	*Citrus maxima* or *Citric grandis* (family Rutaceae)	One of the three original citrus species, rather like an over-sized grapefruit, its white flesh is sweet and pink flesh is sour. Also called pummelo, pamplemousse or shaddock.
Ponderosa lemon	*Citrus maxima medica*	A large, course lemon, a lemon / citron hybrid, grown more as a pot plant than for fruit.
Primofiori lemon (Fino, Mesero)	*Citrus limon* L. Burm. fil	Originally cultivated in Murcia, Spain. Very thorny tree. Fruit with good juice and acid content. Most popular lemon in Spain.
Rangpur lemandarin	*Citrus limonia*	Hybrid between mandarin orange and lemon. High acid content, used as substitute for lime in cooking.

Common Name	Taxonomic Name	Notes / description
Red lime, Rangpur	*Citrus limonia*	Unusual bears mandarin-like red fruit.
Robertson navel	*Citrus sinensis*	Tree lacks vigour, but is very prolific. Popular as a container-grown patio tree.
Rough lemon	*Citrus jambhiri* lush	A lemon citron hybrid, used as a rootstock for sweet orange, mandarin orange and grapefruit.
Round lime, Australian lime	*Citrus australis*	Native to north east Australia, called "Dooja" by indigenous people, slightly pear shaped, rough skinned, used for preserves in Queensland.
Sanguinello	*Citrus sinensis* (L.) Osbeck	Blood orange discovered in Spain.
Santa Teresa lemon	*Citrus limon* L. Burm.f.	From Sicily, same as Femminello, parent tree found to be resistant to Mal Secco disease, so cloned.
Satsuma, cold hardy mandarin, Christmas orange, Satsuma orange, Satsuma mandarin, tangerine	*Citrus unshiu*	Easy peel mandarin, loose skin, sweet. Grown in southern Europe, Argentina, Peru and Chile. A favourite in South Africa where called Naartjie in Afrikaans.
Shangjuan or ichang lemon	*Citrus ichangensis c. maxima*	Small, thorny tree produces large fruit resembles cross between lemon and grapefruit. Cold hardy. Originally from east Asia.
Shonan gold	*Citrus flaviculpus hort. Ex Tanaka (Ogonkan) Citrus unshiu*	First cultivated in Japan in 1988, a hybrid of Golden Orange *(Citrus flaviculpus*) Satsuma orange *(Citrus unshiu)* the succulent flesh is tender and sweet. Smooth skinned, easy peel and fragrant.
Sudachi	*Citrus sudachi*	Small, round, green, Japanese sour fruit, not eaten whole, but used a flavouring in place of lemon or lime.
Sweet lime, Mediterranean sweet lemon	*Citrus limetta*	A cultivar of lemon, popular in south Asia, very mild, sweet flavour, low acid content. Commonly used in fruit drinks.
Sweetie grapefruit	*Citrus maxima paradisi*	Hybrid of acidless pomelo and standard March-type grapefruit, very sweet, similar to Oro blanco.

Common Name	Taxonomic Name	Notes / description
Taiwan tangerine, (Hirami lemon, flat lemon)	*Citrus depressa*	Small, green citrus, thin skinned, native of Taiwan and Japan, very sour, used to garnish dishes, make jam or juice.
Tangelo, Honeybell	*Citrus tangelo, Citrus reticulata C maxima* or *Citrus paradisi*	Cross between tangerine and pomelo or grapefruit. Extremely juicy, mild sweet flavour, used in cooking and drinks.
Tangerine	*Citrus tangerina*	Variety of mandarin orange but sweeter. Used in food, peel eaten coated in chocolate. Originally from Tangiers, Morocco.
Tangor	*Citrus reticulata Citrus sinensis*	Hybrid of mandarin orange and sweet orange, also known as Temple orange. Thick rind, easy to peel, bright orange pulp, sour-sweet and full of flavour.
Tarocco	*Citrus sinensis*	Blood orange grown around Mount Etna, Italy.
Ugli fruit	*Citrus reticulata citrus paradisi*	Cross between an orange, grapefruit and tangerine. Large, super juicy, sweet and with very aromatic rind.
Valencia sweet oranges	*Citrus sinensis 'Valencia'*	Hybridised in mid-19th Century in California from pomelo and mandarin orange. Excellent taste, few seeds. Used as both fruit and for processing as juice. Worldwide, Valencia oranges are prized as the only variety of orange in season during summer. One of the most popular oranges, today; as well as the States, also grown in Spain, South Africa and Australia.
Verna lemon	*Citrus limon*	Virtually seedless, with less juice than Eureka, with tender pulp and good acid content.
Villafranca lemon	*Citrus limon* L. Burm.f.	Indistinguishable from Eureka lemon but seasonal distribution of crop more like Lisbon lemon.
Washington navel or Bahia (from Brazil)	*Citrus sinensis*	Not very vigorous tree, seedless, easy peeling, autumn/winter maturity. Not now commercially available in California

Common Name	Taxonomic Name	Notes / description
Yuzu	*Citrus junos* *Citrus ichangensis* *xitrus reticulata*	Highly aromatic, looks like small grapefruit, juice is used but rarely consumed as a fruit.

APPENDIX B – ARTICLE FROM INDIAN RIVER CITRUS MUSEUM, FLORIDA

by Heather Stapleton, Executive Director, Indian River Citrus Museum

Citrus certainly grows well in Florida. The citrus blossom is the Florida State Flower. However, citrus does not naturally occur in Florida, nor anywhere in the New World.

Citrus' journey began in subtropical Southeast Asia, where it is native, then travelled through the Middle East to North Africa, Europe, finally reaching the New World.

Though no one discovered Vitamin C until hundreds of years later, even in the late 1400s, Europeans understood that eating citrus on ships prevented scurvy. As a result, and thanks to a Spanish law requiring their sailors to carry sour orange seeds with them to plant in the New World for medicinal uses, citrus arrived in the Caribbean and Florida in the late 15th Century.

Around 1807, Colonel Thomas Dummitt of the British Marines sailed past Merritt Island while on his way to St. Augustine. According to local legend, Colonel Dummitt was overwhelmed with the aroma of wild orange blossoms as he and his family passed by.

Dummitt and other early settlers recognized the Indian River Lagoon offered ideal local growing conditions for these fruit. From the wild, they collected roots of the sour oranges left behind by the Spanish. These roots were hardy and had adapted to the local conditions, surviving over hundreds of years. The roots were then grafted with the budwood of more delicate sweet oranges, creating a winning combination.

As a result of his military service in the Second Seminole War, Dummitt and his son acquired land through the Florida Armed Occupation Act of 1842. Here he established commercial orange groves on Merritt Island.

The Indian River is a thin 200 mile (320 kilometre) stretch of land near the Indian River Lagoon, from just south of Flagler Beach to West Palm. Today only fruit from this area may be legally referred to as 'Indian River Fruit', a phrase which is protected by the Federal Trade Commission.

In 1894–95 there was a Great Freeze that affected all the State's new orange groves except those in the Indian River District. All other early commercial groves had to begin again – but due to the hardy rootstock of the Dummitt wild oranges and their location, their family groves did not have to be moved further south or replanted.

The reason the Indian River District has not suffered significant damage from any freeze is a result of a combination of factors:

- proximity of the Gulf Stream – the Indian River District juts out into the warm confines of the ocean. (Vero Beach is over 100 miles further east than Jacksonville.)

- cold fronts have to travel a lot further to get to the Indian River Citrus District.

- as cold fronts move south, they are buffered by all of the rivers, swamps, and lakes plus the lagoon itself, which has a huge buffering effect.

- flat topography means that growers can flood groves when a freeze is forecast. Standing water will radiate its heat during the night, raising the grove temperature by two to four degrees, which ensures another buffer against freezing temperatures.

- rootstock used today are descendants of the hardy plants left behind by the Spanish explorers some 500 years ago.

To learn more, visit the Indian River Citrus Museum – just inside the Heritage Center, in historic Downtown Vero at 2140 14th Ave. It's refreshingly interesting. More details from info@veroheritage.org

POST SCRIPT

When I first started to write this book, I was interested in citrus fruit, but had not realised just how much this family of plants impacts all of us. I kept finding links to my own life with this fruit, from the Welfare Orange Juice that I remember drinking as an infant, through the Crown Ducal china with the orange tree design that we used at home for meals when I was a child, to the huge range of mandarins, satsumas and similar that I now eat every day.

I have researched and checked as much as I could to ensure that the information here is correct, having worked on the journalist principle of seeking to verify everything from three independent sources where available. But I am sure to have made some mistakes.

I repeatedly found some conflicting facts and figures, whether it was simply dates or more importantly descriptions, particularly historical incidents. Similarly, information on who grows what, where and how much varies depending on the source of data.

So if you know of facts or other details that I have got wrong, do please let me know, and I will correct things in future editions of this book. Please contact me at: info@abucon.co.uk

- o 0 o -

ACKNOWLEDGEMENTS

I would like to thank all those who have helped me with this book with their many conversations and exchanges of emails in which people have generously given me their time and knowledge about the wonderful world of citrus. I am grateful to those strict, old-fashioned school teachers who instilled in me self-discipline, and encouraged the development of my tenacious nature. As a child, I might have resented their authoritarian attitude, but in time I came to appreciate their guidance. Thanks are also due to all those companies who have agreed that I can publish photos of their products associated with citrus, as well as to my in-house team, Pam and Kirsty, and copy editor/proofreader Deborah.

- o 0 o -

Sitting under a citrus tree in Spain - truly sublime!

Printed in Great Britain
by Amazon

39531469R00124